SOVIET ECONOMIC FACTS
1917–1970

SOVIET ECONOMIC FACTS 1917–1970

ROGER A. CLARKE

Lecturer in Political Economy
University of Glasgow

A HALSTED PRESS BOOK

John Wiley & Sons
New York – Toronto

First published 1972 by
THE MACMILLAN PRESS LTD
London and Basingstoke
Associated companies in New York Toronto Dublin Melbourne Johannesburg and Madras

Published in the U.S.A. and Canada by Halsted Press, a Division of John Wiley & Sons, Inc., New York

Library of Congress Cataloging in Publication Data

Clarke, Roger A.
Soviet economic facts, 1917–1970.

"A Halsted Press book."
Bibliography: p. 145
1. Russia—Economic conditions—1917–
2. Russia—Statistics. I. Title.
HC335.C518 330.9′47′084 72–8938
ISBN 0–470–15891–3

Printed in Great Britain

Contents

III Agriculture

Preface

After a relatively limited amount of experience of using Soviet statistical sources I began to feel that a considerable waste of time was frequently involved in searching for data because one often could not know what particular volume to consult. This is primarily because of the practice of giving not a complete series for, say, the ten years preceding the date of publication, but only statistics from selected past years. Compiling a series for a period of years, therefore, frequently involves reference to several volumes. In addition, the general statistical annuals often need to be supplemented by use of specialised statistical volumes on particular sectors of the economy or other topics. Most of the volumes are also quite unnecessarily repetitious and therefore bulky, making data more difficult to find quickly. For these reasons I started to think about producing one compact volume which would contain the most used and useful data from the whole range of Soviet statistical volumes available, and thus would give as nearly as possible complete annual series.

Such a volume has an obvious function of making Soviet statistical material more accessible to those who read no Russian. Only the small pocket books, *The USSR in Figures*, are regularly published in English in Moscow;* but they have rather limited data, and there are presumably some users or potential users of Soviet statistics who are neither primarily Soviet experts nor Russian-reading. I also hope and think that this volume should be of considerable use to the specialist who does read Russian and could use the Soviet sources: they may not all be available easily, and in addition my aim has been to produce a book which will be a quicker and more convenient source, while having absolutely equivalent authenticity to the Soviet publications.

The object of this volume therefore is to present under one cover

* An English edition of the 1967 *Strana Sovetov za 50 Let—Soviet Union—50 Years*—appeared in 1970, but this is considerably more restricted in coverage than a normal Soviet annual abstract, and certainly does not go far towards fulfilling the aims I set myself.

as nearly as possible complete annual series for the main aggregate economic magnitudes, a list of industrial and agricultural products which is determined basically by availability, and certain other more general data related to economic performance. The volume is compiled exclusively from Soviet original sources so that it can be used as equivalent to the official publications. Each table accordingly cites all the sources from which it has been compiled. There has been no attempt to fill gaps in data by deduction or anything else beyond, in a few cases only, undisputable arithmetical procedures such as calculation of absolute data from percentages in a source, where the base is clearly identifiable. Several items thus remain completely ignored in the volume—e.g. aircraft, ships, non-ferrous metals, income distribution, peasant incomes—since no official data about them are published.

The result of this has been a number of gaps in several of the tables. These occur most frequently for certain periods. In the early 1920s data collection was still primitive and the situation often confused, even after the civil war was over; and data for the civil war period itself would be largely meaningless if they did exist. The late 1930s were affected by Stalin's increasing concern for security and secrecy, and few data were published. The war years are an obvious gap, filled in a few cases from the official Soviet history of the war; but, as with the civil war, the meaningfulness of any data for these years is questionable. Finally, the early post-war years were shrouded in secrecy, and in some cases data were never published later. There are however very few series indeed for which at least data for the past twenty years are not available, and this is probably the period for which statistics are most required by the majority of users.

Much has been written in the West about the reliability of Soviet statistics by authors far more competent to discuss the subject than I, and I do not think it appropriate to try to make any, necessarily brief and inadequate, comment on it in this book. I have however felt it essential to provide notes in certain cases explaining definitions of coverage where this may be unfamiliar to non-specialists in the field. I should perhaps also add that, while the Soviet definition of national income is different from the Western, it is not generally thought now that this affects the rate of change of national income greatly. The index of industrial output is given as it appears in Soviet sources, and I have assumed that readers are aware of the index problems that arise with changing output patterns over time. The current view of this index for recent years is that it seems to overstate growth by a certain amount compared with physical output figures, probably due to distortions in the calculation of machinery output. A few sources on Soviet statistics are noted at the end of the book. The most recent year's data are frequently taken from the official bulletin in *Pravda*, and some of these figures are liable to be subsequently revised when the yearbook appears later; they are thus in some sense provisional. At the end, I have included as an appendix the main targets for the 1971–5 Five-Year Plan. This is the first such plan to give targets for all five years—previously figures were published for the final year only. It seemed that it might be convenient for some users to have these data alongside those on past performance.

Finally, my thanks to various colleagues in Glasgow and elsewhere with whom I discussed this volume in its early stages. Naturally the customary disclaimer of liability on their part for mistakes applies. Last of all, but by no means least, my very sincere thanks to Elizabeth Hunter and Eleanor Robertson for the heroic task of typing the entire volume from manuscript in my notorious handwriting; incredibly, we are still on speaking terms (just)!

R.A.C.

Tables

I. GENERAL

1. POPULATION

	Total (millions)	*Urban (millions)*	*Urban as % of total*	*Rural (millions)*
1870	86·3*	9·5*	11	76·8*
1897 census	106·3			
estimate	124·6[y]	18·4[y]	15	106·2[y]
1914 est., 1 Jan.	139·3[x]	24·7[x]	18	114·6[x]
1920 census, 28 Aug.	130·9	20·8	16	110·1
1923 urban census and est., 15 March	133·5	21·6	16	111·9
1924 est., 1 Jan.	137·6			
1925 est., 1 Jan.	140·6			
1926 est., 1 Jan.	143·8			
census, 17 Dec. 1926	147·0	26·3	18	120·7
1929 1 Jan.	154·3	27·6	18	126·7
1931 est., 1 July	162·1‡	33·6‡	21	128·5‡
1933 est.	165·7‡	40·3‡	24	125·4‡
1939 census, 17 Jan.	170·6	56·1	33	114·5
est.	190·7[y]	60·4[y]	32	130·3[y]

[x] Pre-September 1939 territory [y] present territory
* Probably present territory; source does not specify.
‡ Contemporary estimates shown by 1939 census to have been substantially too high.

1. POPULATION (continued)

	Total (millions)	Urban (millions)	% inc. over previous year	Urban as % of total	Rural (millions)	% inc.
1940 1 Jan. est.	194·1*	63·1		33	131·0	
1950	178·5	69·4		39	109·1	
1951	181·6	73·0	5·2	40	108·6	−0·5
1952	184·8	76·8	5·2	42	108·0	−0·6
1953	188·0	80·2	4·4	43	107·8	−0·2
1954	191·0	83·6	4·2	44	107·4	−0·4
1955	194·4	86·3	3·2	44	108·1	0·7
1956	197·9	88·2	2·2	45	109·7	1·5
1957	201·4	91·4	3·6	45	110·0	0·3
1958	204·9	95·6	4·6	47	109·3	−0·6
1959 15 Jan. census	208·8	100·0	4·6	48	108·8	−0·5
1960 1 Jan. est.	212·4	103·6	3·6	49	108·8	0
1961	216·3	107·9	4·2	50	108·4	−0·4
1962	220·0	111·2	3·1	51	108·8	0·4
1963	223·5	114·4	2·9	51	109·1	0·3
1964	226·7	117·7	2·9	52	109·0	−0·1
1965	229·6	120·7	2·5	53	108·9	−0·1
1966	232·2	123·7	2·5	53	108·5	−0·4
1967	234·8	126·9	2·6	54	107·9	−0·6
1968	237·2	129·8	2·3	55	107·4	−0·5
1969	239·5	132·9	2·4	55	106·6	−0·7
1970 15 Jan. census	241·7	136·0	2·3	56	105·7	−0·8
1971 1 Jan. est.	243·9	139·0	2·2	57	104·9	−0·8
1972	246·3					

Note. The 1966–70 figures are the revised ones first published in *Nar. Khoz. 1969*, adjusted in the light of the 1970 census.

Sources: *Nar. Khoz. SSSR* (1932), 401
Nar. Khoz. 1964, 7; *1965*, 7; *1969*, 7; *1970*, 7
Pravda (23 January 1972)
Sots. stroi. SSSR (1935), xlviii
Sots. stroi. SSSR (1936), 542
Ten Years of Soviet Power in Figures, 1917–27, 32

Note. The first census after the revolution of which full results were published was in 1926. The next was taken in 1937, but no figures ever appeared. It was repeated in 1939, but only very little data was published. The 1959 census was published fully, and the first figures of the 1970 one have appeared.

2. BIRTH, DEATH AND NATURAL INCREASE RATES

(per 1000 of population)

	Births	*Deaths*	*Natural increase*
1913[x]	47·0	30·2	16·8
[y]	45·5	29·1	16·4
1926	44·0	20·3	23·7
1928	44·3	23·3	21·0
1937	38·7	18·9	19·8
1938	37·5	17·5	20·0
1939	36·5	17·3	19·2
1940	31·2	18·0	13·2
1946	23·8	10·8	13·0
1950	26·7	9·7	17·0
1951	27·0	9·7	17·3
1952	26·5	9·4	17·1
1953	25·1	9·1	16·0
1954	26·6	8·9	17·7
1955	25·7	8·2	17·5
1956	25·2	7·6	17·6
1957	25·4	7·8	17·6
1958	25·3	7·2	18·1
1959	25·0	7·6	17·4
1960	24·9	7·1	17·8
1961	23·8	7·2	16·6
1962	22·4	7·5	14·9
1963	21·2	7·2	14·0
1964	19·6	6·9	12·7
1965	18·4	7·3	11·1
1966	18·2	7·3	10·9
1967	17·3	7·6	9·7
1968	17·2	7·7	9·5
1969	17·0	8·1	8·9
1970	17·4	8·2	9·2

[x] Pre-1939 boundaries [y] present boundaries

Sources: *Nar. Khoz. 1969*, 31; *1970*, 47
Strana Sovetov za 50 let (1966), 257
Zdravookhranenie v SSSR (1960), 40

3. NATIONAL INCOME

(produced)

	Index (in constant prices)	*% inc. over previous year*		*Index (in constant prices)*	*% inc. over previous year*
1913	**100**	..	1940	**100**	
1917	71	..	1941	92	− 8·0
1920	40		1942	66	−28·3
1921	38	−5·0	1943	74	12·1
1926	103		1944	88	18·9
1927	110	6·8	1945	83	− 5·7
1928	119	8·2	1946	78	− 6·0
1929	138	16·0	1949	136	
1930	167	21·0	1950	164	20·6
1931	195	16·8	1951	184	12·2
1932	217	11·3	1952	204	10·9
1933	231	6·5	1953	224	9·8
1934	266	15·2	1954	251	12·1
1935	317	19·2	1955	281	12·0
1936	410	29·3	1956	313	11·4
1937	459	12·0	1957	334	6·7
1938	500	8·9	1958	376	12·6
1940	611		1959	404	7·4
			1960	435	7·7
			1961	465	6·9
			1962	491	5·6
			1963	511	4·1
			1964	559	9·4
			1965	597	6·8
			1966	645	8·1
			1967	699	8·4
			1968	759	8·6
			1969	795	4·7
			1970	866	8·9

Note. The pre-1940 index seems to be based on the uncorrected crop figures of the time (see table 60 on Grain Output, p. 110), not the corrected ones, which however are the basis of table 5 on Gross Agricultural Production, p. 10.

Sources: *Bol'shaya Sovetskaya Entsiklopediya*, 2nd ed., 29, 302
Istoriya Velikoi otechestvennoi voiny, 1941–45, VI, 45 (war years)
Nar. Khoz. 1967, 671; *1969*, 557; *1970*, 533

3. NATIONAL INCOME (continued)
(produced)
(*in current prices*)

	(*mlrd rubles*)	% *inc. over previous year*
1960	145·0	7·7
1961	152·9	6·8
1962	164·6	5·7
1963	168·8	4·0
1964	181·3	9·3
1965	193·5	6·9
1966	207·4	8·1
1967	225·5	8·6
1968	244·1	8·3
1969	261·9	4·8
1970	289·6	9·0

Source: *Nar. Khoz. 1970*, 533

4. GROSS INDUSTRIAL PRODUCTION
(index and annual % increase)

	Total		Producer goods		Consumer goods	
	Index	*% inc. over previous year*	*Index*	*% inc. over previous year*	*Index*	*% inc. over previous year*
1913	**100**		**100**		**100**	
1917	71		81		67	
1921	31		29		33	
1924	45		52		41	
1925	73	62·2	80	53·8	69	68·3
1926	98	34·2	113	41·3	90	30·4
1927	111	13·3	128	13·3	102	13·3
1928	132	18·9	155	21·1	120	17·6
1929	158	19·7	200	29·0	137	14·2
1930	193	22·2	276	38·0	151	10·2
1931	233	20·7	355	28·6	171	13·2
1932	267	14·6	424	19·4	187	9·4
1933	281	5·2	450	6·1	196	4·8
1934	335	19·2	563	25·1	220	12·2
1935	411	22·7	713	26·6	258	17·3
1936	529	28·7	934	31·0	324	25·6
1937	588	11·2	1013	8·5	373	15·1
1938	657	11·7	1138	12·3	415	11·3
1939	763	16·1	1353	18·9	464	11·8
1940	852	11·7	1554	14·9	497	7·1
1940	**100**		**100**		**100**	
1941	98	– 2·0	(140, 94)*			
1942	77	–21·4	(186, 53)*			
1943	90	16·9	(224, 59)*		54	
1944	104	15·6	136 (251, 75)*			

* Figures in brackets are for arms and fuel industries respectively.

4. GROSS INDUSTRIAL PRODUCTION (continued)
(index and annual % increase)

	Total		Producer goods		Consumer goods	
	Index	*% inc. over previous year*	*Index*	*% inc. over previous year*	*Index*	*% inc. over previous year*
1945	92	−15·3	112	−17·6	59	9·3
1946	77	−16·3	82	−26·8	67	13·6
1947	93	20·8	101	23·2	82	22·3
1948	118	26·9	130	28·7	99	20·7
1949	141	19·5	163	25·4	107	8·1
1950	173	22·7	205	25·8	123	15·0
1951	202	16·8	239	16·6	143	16·3
1952	225	11·4	268	12·1	158	10·5
1953	252	12·0	299	11·6	177	12·0
1954	285	13·1	340	13·7	200	13·0
1955	320	12·3	390	14·7	217	8·5
1956	354	10·6	434	11·3	237	9·2
1957	390	10·2	481	10·8	256	8·0
1958	430	10·3	536	11·4	277	8·2
1959	479	11·4	602	12·3	304	9·7
1960	524	9·4	666	10·6	326	7·2
1961	572	9·2	735	10·4	348	6·7
1962	627	9·6	814	10·7	374	7·5
1963	678	8·1	891	9·5	393	5·1
1964	728	7·4	970	8·9	408	3·8
1965	791	8·7	1056	8·9	442	8·3
1966	860	8·7	1153	9·2	475	7·5
1967	946	10·0	1269	10·1	522	9·9
1968	1024	8·2	1375	8·4	566	8·4
1969	1097	7·1	1471	7·0	608	7·4
1970	1190	8·5	1593	8·3	662	8·9
1971	1283	7·8	1716	7·7	714	7·9

Sources: *Istoriya . . . 1941–45*, VI, 45 (war years)
Nar. Khoz. 1959, 141; *1969*, 144; *1970*, 130 *Pravda* (23 January 1972)

5. GROSS AGRICULTURAL PRODUCTION

	Total		*Crops*		*Livestock*	
	Index	*% inc. over previous year*	*Index*	*% inc. over previous year*	*Index*	*% inc. over previous year*
1913	**100**	..	**100**	..	**100**	..
1917	88	..	81	..	100	..
1920	67	..	64	..	72	..
1921	60	−10·4	55	−14·1	67	− 6·9
1922	75	25·0	75	36·4	73	9·0
1923	86	14·7	84	12·0	88	20·5
1924	90	4·7	82	− 2·4	104	18·2
1925	112	24·4	107	30·5	121	16·3
1926	118	5·4	114	6·5	127	5·0
1927	121	2·5	113	− 0·9	134	5·5
1928	124	2·5	117	3·5	137	2·2
1929	121	− 2·4	116	− 0·9	129	− 5·8
1930	117	− 3·3	126	8·6	100	−22·5
1931	114	− 2·6	126	0	93	− 7·0
1932	107	− 6·1	125	− 0·8	75	−19·4
1933	101	− 5·6	121	− 3·2	65	−13·3
1934	106	5·0	125	3·3	72	10·8
1935	119	12·3	138	10·4	86	19·4
1936	109	− 8·4	118	−14·5	96	11·6
1937	134	22·9	150	27·1	109	13·5
1938	120	−10·5	120	−20·0	120	10·1
1939	121	0·8	125	4·2	119	− 1·7
1940	141	16·5	155	24·0	114	− 4·2
1940	**100**	..	**100**	..	**100**	..
1941	62	−38·0				
1942	38	−38·7				
1943	37	− 2·6				
1944	54	45·9				

5. GROSS AGRICULTURAL PRODUCTION (continued)

	Total		*Crops*		*Livestock*	
	Index	*% inc. over previous year*	*Index*	*% inc. over previous year*	*Index*	*% inc. over previous year*
1945	60	11·1	57	..	64	..
1946	68	13·3	65	14·0	76	18·8
1947	87	27·9	91	40·0	78	2·6
1948	97	11·5	102	12·1	84	7·7
1949	99	2·1	101	– 1·0	95	13·1
1950	99	0	97	– 4·0	104	9·5
1951	93	– 6·1	86	–11·3	110	5·8
1952	101	8·6	96	11·6	113	2·7
1953	104	3·0	96	0	124	9·7
1954	109	4·8	99	3·1	134	8·1
1955	121	11·0	113	14·1	140	4·5
1956	137	13·2	130	15·0	155	10·7
1957	141	2·9	128	– 1·5	172	11·0
1958	156	10·6	147	14·8	180	4·7
1959	157	0·6	140	– 4·8	194	7·8
1960	160	1·9	147	5·0	193	– 0·5
1961	165	3·1	149	1·4	202	4·7
1962	167	1·2	149	0	207	2·5
1963	155	– 7·2	136	– 8·7	194	– 6·3
1964	177	14·2	175	28·7	191	– 1·5
1965	180	1·7	161	– 8·0	223	16·8
1966	196	8·9	182	13·0	232	4·0
1967	199	1·5	183	0·5	239	3·0
1968	208	4·5	195	6·6	244	2·1
1969	201	– 3·4	182	– 6·7	244	0
1970	221	10·0	204	12·1	265	8·6
1971		0				

Note. Coverage is of pre-1939 territory for 1917–39 inclusive; present territory for 1940 on.

Sources: *Istoriya . . . 1941–45*, VI, 45 (war years)
Nar. Khoz. 1969, 289; *1970*, 275 *Pravda* (23 January 1972)
Sel. Khoz. SSSR (1960), 79

6. INVESTMENT*

(*mlrd. rubles (new), constant 1955 prices*)

	Total	*Total state*	*State centralised*	*Kolkhoz*	*Industry (all sources)*	*Agriculture (all sources)*
	1918–28 (exc. 4th quarter), 4·1		1918–28 (exc. 4th quarter), 1·674		1918–28 (exc. 4th quarter) 0·631	1918–28 (exc. 4th quarter) 0·114
1928	4th quarter 1928–1932 inc., 7·3	0·828		0·038	4th quarter 1928–32 inc. 2·76	4th quarter 1928–32 inc. 1·13
1929			0·794			
1930		1·39	1·32	0·106		
1931		2·02	1·90	0·083		
1932		2·35	2·20	0·078		
1933	1933–7 inc., 16·6	1·94	1·79	0·119	1933–7 inc. 6·16	1933–7 inc. 2·01
1934		2·55	2·37	0·137		
1935		2·98	2·78	0·188		
1936		4·07	3·84	0·251		
1937		3·62	3·44	0·298		
1938	1938–1st half 1941 inc., 17·3	3·81	3·62	0·302	1938–1st half 1941 inc. 5·92	1938–1st half 1941 inc. 1·88
1939		4·43	4·15	0·362		
1940	2nd half 1941–5 inc., 17·5	4·73	4·45	0·436	2nd half 1941–5 inc. 7·44	2nd half 1941–5 inc. 1·65
1941		4·07	3·96	0·334		
1942		2·49	2·45	0·242		
1943		2·50	2·44	0·304		
1944		3·41	3·33	0·427		

* Total state investment means all investment financed by state institutions and enterprises, i.e. excluding collective farms and private individuals. State centralised investment is that part (the largest part) of state investment which is allocated by the central planning authorities; other state investment is by enterprises and institutions using the resources left at their own disposal for this purpose. The difference between the sum of total state and *kolkhoz* (collective farm) investment and the overall total is accounted for by private investment in house-building. The figures given for industry and agriculture are for all sources of finance, but are for productive investment pertaining to these sectors' output, excluding, for example, construction of cultural amenities by industrial enterprises or farms.

(mlrd rubles (new), constant 1955 prices)

	Total	Total state	State centralised	Kolkhoz	Industry (all sources)	Agriculture (all sources)
1945	1946–50 inc., 41·2	4·21*	4·09	0·399	1946–50 inc. 15·7	1946–50 inc. 5·0
1946		5·04*	4·81	0·521		
1947		5·47*	5·13	0·642		
1948		6·63*	6·33	0·673		
1949		8·11*	7·63	0·563		
1950	10·9	9·4	9·21	0·751	4·18	1·66
1951	1951–5 inc., 77·7	10·6	10·3	0·921		1·86
1952		11·9	11·6	1·1	(6·4)†	1·93
1953		12·5	12·1	1·2	1951–5 inc. 31·4	1·91
1954		14·6	14·1	1·4		1951–5 inc. 11·6; 2·76
1955		16·1	15·2	2·1	31·4	3·80
1956	22·4	18·6	17·1	2·3	(9·4)†	4·02
1957	25·3	21·1	19·1	2·2	(9·9)†	4·20
1958	29·4	23·9	20·6	2·8	10·0(11·2)†	4·71
1959	33·3	26·7	22·9	3·5	(13·0)†	5·07
1960	35·9	30·0	25·8	3·2	12·7(14·3)†	5·16
1961	37·5	31·9	28·1	3·2	13·1	5·35
1962	39·3	34·0	30·4	3·3	14·0	5·94
1963	41·3	36·1	32·4	3·4	14·9	6·55
1964	45·0	39·4	34·9	3·9	16·7	7·82
1965	48·7	42·7	37·0	4·3	17·7	8·57
1966	§61·0 / 52·4	§53·7 / 45·8	§45·6 / 39·0	§5·6 / 4·9	§21·8 / 18·3	§10·1 / 9·39
1967	66·0 / 56·7	58·0 / 49·4	48·0 / 41·0	6·4 / 5·6	23·3 / 19·5	10·8 / 10·0
1968	71·2 / 61·4	62·5 / 53·5	50·4 / 43·1	7·1 / 6·2	25·2 / 21·3	12·1 / 11·2
1969	73·6 / 63·4	65·1 / 55·8	52·3 / 44·9	6·8 / 5·9	26·2 / 22·0	12·6 / 11·7
1970	82·0	72·7	57·2	7·7	29·6	14·2

* 1945–9 total state figures have slightly different coverage from subsequent years (on previous units, 1950 figure is 9·6).
† The figures in brackets are on a slightly different coverage.
§ These higher figures are in the revised prices of 1967. The statistics appeared in the old prices until 1969, but the 1970 *Nar. Khoz.* showed them recalculated.

Sources: *Nar. Khoz. 1961*, 537–8; *1965*, 528, 529, 530; *1969*, 501, 503, 504–5; *1970*, 478, 481, 482–3
Kapital'noe stroitel'stvo v SSSR, stat. sbor. (1961), 51, 155

7. PRICES (indices)

	State retail trade (including public catering)						Urban kolkhoz markets (excluding cattle)	
	All goods		Food		Non-food			
1940		**100**		**100**		**100**	**100**	
1947 (4th quarter)	**100**		**100**		**100**			
1948	83		82		86			
1949 (i:iii)	71		68		78			
1950 (i:iii)	57	186	53	203	65	165	98	
1951 (i:iii)	53	170	48	181	63	157		
1952 (i:iv)	50	161	43	166	62	156		
1953		146		146		145		
1954		138		141		134	110	
1955		138		141		134	112	
1956		138		143		133	100	
1957		138		143		133	98	
1958		141		149		133	106	
1959		140		148		132	102	
1960		139		147		130	108	**100**
1961		138		146		129	117	108
1962		140		150		129	128	118
1963		141		153		129	144	134
1964		141		152		128	152	141
1965		140		152		126	127	118
1966		139		151		124	129	119
1967		139		151		124	129	119
1968		139		151		124	137*	127*
1969		139		152		124		
1970		139		152		124		

* Since 1968 *kolkhoz* market trade data have ceased to appear.

Note. Price indices are not given in the official statistical handbooks for most of the prewar period. Using archive materials a Soviet scholar, A. Malafeyev, in *Istoriya tsenoobrazovaniya v SSSR* (Moscow 1964), calculated an index for prices in state and co-operative retail trade of 255 for 1932 (1928=100). The rise in free market prices was very much greater; in the first half of 1932 they were on average 769% above the levels of 1927–8. He calculated that from 1932 to 1937 state and co-operative prices of all types taken together rose on average by 110·2%, but since free market prices fell (1932, 100; 1933, 148·2; 1934, 90·8; 1935, 64·6; 1936, 55·3; 1937, 62·3), he calculated the overall retail price index for 1937 as 80% above 1932.

Sources: *Nar. Khoz. 1959*, 677, 710; *1960*, 716, 739; *1968*, 639, 655; *1970*, 602
Sovetskaya Torgovlya (1956), 131, 132, 183
The *kolkhoz* market indices have been recalculated from several *Nar. Khoz.* volumes: *1962*, 532, 543; *1963*, 539; *1964*, 647, 659; *1967*, 739.

8. INTERNAL TRADE

Turnover

(*mlrd new (1961) rubles, in current prices*)

	Total state and co-operative retail trade inc. public catering	*of which retail trade*	*% food in total*	*% urban in total*	*kolkhoz market trade*
1924	0·29	0·27		74	
1925	0·51	0·49		71	
1926	0·76	0·73		70	
1927	0·94	0·91		67	
1928	1·18	1·14	48·1	67	
1929	1·52	1·46		67	
1930	1·89	1·76		64	
1931	2·79	2·52		68	
1932	4·04	3·55	55·1	68	0·750
1933	4·98	4·34	58·8	71	1·15
1934	6·18	5·48	62·3	74	1·40
1935	8·17	7·45	65·4	72	1·45
1936	10·68	9·88		70	
1937	12·59	11·58	63·1	69	
1938	14·00	12·74	62·9	70	2·44
1939	16·58	14·93	63·1	69	
1940	17·51	15·22	63·1	71	2·91
1945	16·01	12·70	75·6	74	
1946	24·72	19·84	74·5	77	
1947	33·08	26·27	71·9	82	
1948	31·02	26·47	64·4	80	
1949	33·51	28·96	61·4	77	
1950	35·96	31·22	58·4	76	4·92
1951	37·98	32·96	57·8	75	5·08
1952	39·36	34·02	57·3	75	5·37
1953	43·07	37·36	55·1	75	4·88
1954	48·19	42·19	54·8	74	5·10

8. **INTERNAL TRADE** (continued)

Turnover (continued)

(mlrd new (1961) rubles, in current prices)

	Total state and co-operative retail trade, inc. public catering	*of which retail trade*	*% food in total*	*% urban in total*	*kolkhoz market trade*
1955	50·19	44·31	54·9	73	5·23
1956	54·74	48·70	54·7	73	4·81
1957	62·50	56·19	54·0	74	4·66
1958	67·72	61·29	54·6	74	4·84
1959	71·92	65·48	54·6	75	4·62
1960	78·56	71·53	54·4	76	4·34
1961	81·08	73·66	55·3	76	4·66
1962	87·30	79·21	56·2	76	5·27
1963	91·69	82·92	57·9	77	4·98
1964	96·36	86·74	58·2	77	5·23
1965	104·76	94·70	57·7	77	4·95
1966	113·02	102·29	57·4	77	5·10
1967	123·58	111·94	57·0	77	5·32
1968	134·19	121·45	56·2	77	5·51
1969	144·40	130·38	55·9	78	
1970	155·21	140·18	55·5	77	

Note. Since all these figures are in current prices, and the level of *kolkhoz* market prices has typically been higher (at times very much higher) than state retail prices, they do not give accurate figures for the share of this trade.

Sources: *Nar. Khoz. 1959,* 637, 642, 708; *1960*, 736; *1962*, 540; *1964*, 657; *1968*, 613, 614, 617, 654; *1970*, 577, 581
Sovetskaya Torgovlya (1956), 21, 39, 179
Sots. stroi. Soyuza SSR 1933–8, 110; *1936*, 606

9. FOOD CONSUMPTION PER HEAD

1. Whole population

(*kilogrammes per annum*)

	Meat and animal fat (inc. poultry and fresh subproducts)	*Milk and milk products (in milk equivalent)*	*Eggs (number)*	*Fish and fish products*	*Sugar*	*Vegetable oil*	*Potatoes*	*Vegetables and pulses*	*Grain products (bread,* flour, groats, beans, macaroni)*
1913	29	154	48	6·7	8·1	—	114	40	200
1950	26	172	60	7·0	11·6	2·7	241	51	172
1958	36	238	108	9·8	24·2	4·7	150	71	172
1960	40	240	118	9·9	28·0	5·3	143	70	164
1964	38	238	113	12·2	32·2	6·6	140	74	159
1965	41	251	124	12·6	34·2	7·1	142	72	156
1966	44	260	132	12·9	35·3	6·3	135	73	153
1967	46	274	138	13·2	36·7	6·5	131	80	150
1968	48	285	144	14·3	37·4	6·5	131	79	149
1969	47	304	148	15·8	37·8	6·6	131	76	149
1970	48	307	158	15·4	38·8	6·8	130	83	149

* Bread expressed as flour equivalent.

Sources: *Nar. Khoz. 1965*, 597; *1967*, 697; *1968*, 595; *1969*, 583; *1970*, 561

9. FOOD CONSUMPTION PER HEAD (continued)

2. State-employed labour force

(*kilogrammes per annum*)

	Meat and animal fat (inc. poultry and fresh subproducts)	*Milk and milk products (in milk equivalent)*	*Eggs (number)*	*Fish and fish products*	*Sugar*	*Vegetable oil*	*Potatoes*	*Vegetables and pulses*	*Grain products (bread,* flour, groats, beans, macaroni)*
1960	44	245	117	12·0	32·4	5·9	132	74	153
1965	43	257	124	14·4	36·7	7·4	135	78	149
1966	46	265	131	14·5	37·6	6·5	129	79	145
1967	49	279	137	14·8	38·5	6·8	125	85	143
1968	51	290	143	15·9	38·8	6·7	125	83	142

* Bread expressed as flour equivalent.

Note. Some index figures for the period before 1960 (post-war) are published, but they are for the 'workers' section of the state-employed labour force only, and cannot therefore be combined with the post-1960 figures for the whole state-employed labour force, as the difference in coverage is obviously large.

Source: *Nar. Khoz. 1967*, 697; *1968*, 595

9. FOOD CONSUMPTION PER HEAD (continued)

3. Collective farm members

(*kilogrammes per annum*)

	Meat and animal fat (inc. poultry and fresh subproducts)	*Milk and milk products (in milk equivalent)*	*Eggs (number)*	*Fish and fish products*	*Sugar*	*Vegetable oil*	*Potatoes*	*Vegetables and pulses*	*Grain products (bread,* flour, groats, beans, macaroni)*
1940	16	142	42	1·7	2·5		137	46	202
1952	13	149	47	2·3	4·9		224	41	192
1953	18	156	59	2·6	7·1		214	54	198
1954	21	166	72	3·0	9·0		188	57	198
1955	23	188	82	3·7	6·8		191	57	201
1956	26	210	89	4·1	10·8		191	58	202
1957	29	218	107	4·4	12·3		190	56	198
1958	30	232	111	4·9	14·2		171	59	198
1959	32	232	119	5·2	17·4		171	55	194
1960	30	228	122	5·4	18·2	4·1	168	59	188
1965	33	234	123	7·1	26·5	6·1	161	56	177
1966	35	246	133	7·9	28·3	5·4	154	56	176
1967	37	260	141	8·2	31·2	5·8	148	65	172
1968	37	268	146	9·0	32·9	6·0	151	65	172

* Bread expressed in flour equivalent.

Note. 1940–59 figures calculated from indices in sources.

Sources: *Nar. Khoz. 1956*, 219; *1959*, 715; *1960*, 742; *1967*, 697; *1968*, 595

10. CONSUMER DURABLES—STOCKS

(*per 1000 of population*)

(*at end of year*)	*1960*	*1965*	*1966*	*1967*	*1968*	*1969*	*1970*
Watches and clocks	794	885	897	902	922	935	958
Radio sets (inc. radiograms)	129	165	170	177	186	193	199
TV sets	22	68	81	96	112	127	143
Cameras	49	67	70	73	75	76	80
Bicycles, mopeds	116	134	139	141	143	144	148
Motorcycles	10	17	18	19	20	20	21
Vacuum cleaners	8	18	20	22	25	28	31
Sewing machines	107	144	148	150	154	157	161
Refrigerators	10	29	37	47	58	71	87
Washing machines	13	59	73	89	106	123	139

Sources: *Nar. Khoz. 1967*, 584; *1968*, 596; *1970*, 562

11. HOUSING

Area completed

(m. square yards of total (useful) space)

	Total (urban and rural) state, co-operative, kolkhoz and private	*Total urban*	*Total state and co-operative (urban and rural)*	*Urban private*	*Rural private and kolkhoz*
1918–28	203·0		23·7		
1929–32	56·9		32·6		
1933–7	67·3		37·2		
1938–41 (1st half)	81·6		34·4		
1941 (2nd half) –5	102·5		41·3		
1946–50 (inc. reconstruction)	200·9		72·4		
1946			12·6		
1947			11·8		
1948			14·7		
1949			15·5		
1950			17·8		
1951–5	240·5		113·0		
1951			20·3		
1952			20·0		
1953			23·2		
1954			24·5		
1955			25·0		
1956–60	474·1		224·0		
1956			29·5		
1957			38·5		
1958			46·7		
1959			53·5		

11. HOUSING (continued)

Area completed (continued)

(m. square yards of total (useful) space)

	Total (urban and rural) state, co-operative, kolkhoz and private	*Total urban*	*Total state and co-operative (urban and rural)*	*Urban private*	*Rural private and kolkhoz*
1960	109·6	59·0	55·8	14·4	39·4
1961	102·7	56·1	56·6	12·4	33·7
1962	100·0	58·9	59·8	11·4	28·8
1963	97·6	58·4	61·9	9·8	25·9
1964	92·7	57·5	58·9	9·2	24·6
1965	97·6	60·7	63·2	8·0	26·4
1966	102·1	63·4	65·9	7·7	28·5
1967	104·5	66·1	68·7	7·8	28·0
1968	102·1	66·1	69·3	7·2	25·6
1969	103·8	68·6	72·0	7·1	24·7
1970	106·0	71·3	76·6	6·6	22·8
1971	over 108				

Notes. Before 1966 statistics for houses built on *kolkhozy*, both by the *kolkhozy* and privately, were published in numbers of houses, not in area, and data on these expressed in area have only appeared for years back to 1960.

Cols. 3, 4 and 5 add up to col. 1.

Figures for rural private and *kolkhoz* separately are not available.

Sources: *Nar. Khoz. 1962*, 498; *1958*, 636; *1962*, 498; *1968*, 573, 574; *1969*, 562; *1970*, 538–9
Pravda (23 January 1972)

12. LABOUR FORCE

1. Total state-employed

(millions)

	Total	% women		Total	% women
1913[x]	11·4		1948	35·8	
[y]	12·9		1949	37·6	
1920	5·0		1950	40·4	47
			1951	42·3	48
1924	7·4		1952	43·9	48
1925	8·6		1953	45·4	48
1926	10·0		1954	49·1	46
1927	10·7		1955	50·3	46
1928	11·4	24	1956	51·9	45
1929	12·4	27	1957	54·5	46
1930	15·4	27	1958	56·0	46
1931	20·2	27	1959	57·9	47
1932	24·2	27	1960	62·0	47
1933	23·5	30	1961	65·9	48
1934	24·8	32	1962	68·3	48
1935	25·9	33	1963	70·5	48
1936	27·2		1964	73·3	49
1937	28·6		1965	76·9	49
1938	29·9		1966	79·7	50
1939	31·6		1967	82·3	50
1940	33·9	39	1968	85·1	50
			1969	87·9	51
1945	28·6	56			
1946	32·0		1970	90·2	51
1947	33·5		1971	92·7	

[x] Pre-1939 territory [y] Present territory

Sources: *Nar. Khoz. 1969*, 530, 537; *1970*, 509, 517
Pravda (23 January 1972)
Trud v SSSR (1936), 25 (for percentages women, 1928–35. The absolute labour force figures in this volume differ from those in the 1968 source).
Trud v SSSR (1968), 22, 73

12. LABOUR FORCE (continued)

2. State-employed labour force by sectors*

	Industry	*Agri-culture*	*Annual average number on kolkhozy*	*Forestry*	*Trans-port*	*Com-munica-tions*	*Con-struction*
1928	4,339	1660	0·8	75	1302	95	749
1932	9,374	2949		100	2146	224	2313
1937	11,641	2609		248	2764	375	1604
1940	13,079	2703	29·0	280	3525	484	1620
1945	10,665	2731	23·5	199	3126	426	1527
1950	15,317	3437	27·6	444	4117	542	2603
1951	16,230						2692
1952	16,873	(3693)		462	4595	565	2809
1953	17,617	4026		416	(4770)	582	2870
1954	18,499						3202
1955	18,868	6157	24·8	389	{ 5056 (5039)	611	3210
1956	19,561	6095		390	(5216)	624	3567
1957	20,192	6793		377	(5355)	641	4017
1958	20,807	6195		367	5681	664	4442
1959	21,400			352	5972	691	4800
1960	22,620	7123	22·3	359	6279	738	5143
1961	23,475	7838	20·7	378	6518	790	5270
1962	24,297	8197	20·0	389	6677	832	5150
1963	25,057	8339	19·4	399	6841	877	5237
1964	25,933	8552	19·2	404	7054	928	5370
1965	27,447	8704	18·9	402	7252	1007	5685
1966	28,514	8894	18·6	409	7364	1073	5871
1967	29,448	8836		412	7467	1123	6124
1968	30,428	8903	18·0	421	7606	1187	6342
1969	31,159	9083	17·2	426	7803	1260	6651
1970	31,593	9180	16·7	433	7985	1330	6994

* Figures in brackets are not fully comparable, but are the only ones available; the coverage seems to have been changed around 1965.

† Includes Arts in all years, but source lists this separately for 1969.

Note. The state-employed labour force consists of all employed people except members of collective farms, who are not technically state employees but members of a voluntary co-operative. The total state-employed labour force is thus substantially less than the total working population. The figures for the labour force by sectors include all people employed in the sectors irrespective of profession; e.g., all people working in schools, from headmasters to cleaners, are counted under education. For agriculture the figures for state-employed relate mostly to state farms. In addition, therefore, we give the annual average number of *kolkhoz* members. This includes a small number doing non-agricultural work, but it also excludes work on the private plots. The total of these two columns is thus considerably less

	Trade, public catering, supply and procurements	*Housing and communal services*	*Health and social insurance*	*Education and culture*	*Science and scientific services*	*Credit and state insurance*	*State, economic, co-operative and social administration*	*Other sectors*
1928	606	158	399	725	82	95	1010	149
1932	2223	711	669	1292	145	128	1650	303
1937	2551	1102	1127	2088	279	193	1488	494
1940	3351	1516	1512	2678	362	267	1837	712
1945	2445	1046	1419	2352	289	197	1645	499
1950	3360	1371	2051	3315	714	264	1831	1054
1952	3495	(1315)	2226	3553	829	262	1786	(1079)
1953	(3463)	(1345)	2308	3647	860	263	1726	(1150)
1955	3756 (3725)	1583 (1400)	2627	3988	992	265	1361	1388 (1269)
1956	(3826)	(1503)	2736	4103	1094	266	1342	(1292)
1957	(4017)	(1579)	2892	4250	1208	266	1294	(1337)
1958	4190	1754	3059	4378	1338	260	1294	1576
1959	4389	(1713)	3245	4556	1474	260	1273	(1739)
1960	4675	1920	3461	4803	1763	265	1245	1968
1961	5010	2030	3677	5165	2011	277	1295	2127
1962	5253	2096	3818	5521	2213	283	1316	2236
1963	5487	2182	3933	5835	2370	289	1308	2372
1964	5752	2282	4082	6204	2497	296	1354	2550
1965	6009	2386	4277	6600	2625	300	1460	2761
1966	6261	2489	4427	6895	2741	313	1546	2912
1967	6575	2674	4545	7172	2850	329	1651	3068
1968	6964	2800	4747	7507	2990	345	1744	3116
1969	7287	2930	4927	7777	3128	363	1834	3298†
1970	7537	3052	5080	8025	3238	388	1883	

than the total labour input into agriculture, because of the exclusion of the private plots, and also because it excludes labour temporarily directed to agriculture from other sectors at harvest time; this latter was 0·5 million (in annual average equivalent) in 1966.

All the above remarks apply also to the tables following on wages. The national average thus excludes *kolkhoz* members. Figures for average annual earnings of *kolkhoz* members are not published, either for pay from the farms or for earnings from their private plots. Because of the definition of sectors used, the figures give only a very rough indication of, for example, the relative trend of teachers' and industrial workers' pay.

Sources: *Nar. Khoz. 1958*, 658–9; *1962*, 453–4; *1964*, 546–7; *1965*, 558–9; *1968*, 548–9; *1969*, 397, 530–1; *1970*, 382, 510–11
Strana Sovetov za 50 Let, 218–19
Trud v SSSR (1968), 24–5, 81, 121, 124–5

13. WAGES

1. Annual money average for state-employed labour force*
(current (pre-war) rubles)

					Transport				
	Total	*Large-scale industry*	*Small-scale industry*	*Construction*	*Total*	*Rail*	*Water*	*Other*	*Agriculture (inc. forestry and fishing)*
1923/24	—	456	369	537	386	375	460	403	—
1924/25	450	566	459	676	529	514	627	554	201
1925/26	571	701	506	826	715	710	707	741	250
1926/27	624	778	561	911	787	786	799	782	267
1928	703	870	637	996	861	859	904	846	313
1929	800	957	680	1025	929	906	1031	984	399
1930	936	1035	823	1082	1064	1030	1162	1147	547
1931	1127	1184	1037	1243	1196	1159	1273	1279	799
1932	1427	1473	1251	1509	1506	1496	1509	1539	940
1933	1566	1662	1486	1641	1672	1637	1709	1738	1082
1934	1858	1927	1528	2042	1954	1930	2103	1961	1287
1935	2269	2375	1680	2497	2389	2311	2533	2507	1575
1938	3467								

	Com-munications	*Trade*	*Public catering*	*Credit*	*Education*	*Health*	*Administra-tion*	*Communal enterprises*	*Domestic and casual*
1923/24	402	616	568	789	—	—	—	399	152
1924/25	499	641	586	807	389	413	564	486	187
1925/26	615	746	561	914	509	500	750	603	220
1926/27	712	760	591	920	544	569	818	607	236
1928	776	783	623	981	678	638	903	696	251
1929	721	798	733	971	788	727	1020	712	400
1930	760	893	778	1199	978	799	1170	814	431
1931	1029	1071	837	1518	1253	938	1471	1099	483
1932	1333	1351	1059	1834	1633	1248	1943	1453	828
1933	1450	1343	1122	2128	1765	1413	2354	1529	784
1934	1571	1483	1242	2336	1941	1545	2694	1663	849
1935	1944	1851	1552	2664	2328	2249	3246	1964	1074

* See table 12 Note.

Sources: *Trud v SSSR* (1936), 16–17   *Sots. Stroi Soyuza SSSR 1933–38*, 139 (for 1938 total figure)

13. **WAGES** (continued)

2. Monthly money average for state-employed labour force (continued)

(*current* (*new*) *rubles*)

	Total state-employed	*Industry total*	*Industrial workers*	*State farms*	*1 Total transport*	*2 Rail transport*	*3 Water transport*	*4 Road, urban electric and other transport, and loaders*	*Com-munications*
1940	33·0	34·0	32·3	21·9	34·7	34·1	40·9	34·5	28·1
1945	43·4	47·0	45·0	21·3	48·2	52·5	49·3	40·9	35·4
1946	47·5								
1950	63·9	70·3	68·7	38·2	70·5	72·5	78·6	67·3	52·7
1955	71·5	78·3	76·2	46·6	77·0	77·5	90·6	74·9	55·6
1956	73·4								
1957	76·2								
1958	77·8	87·1	85·3	53·1	82·2	80·7	97·9	81·8	58·0
1959	79·0								
1960	80·1	91·3	89·8	53·9	86·7	82·4	106·0	87·8	62·3
1961	83·4	94·5	92·7	58·0	93·1	90·3	121·2	92·5	70·6
1962	86·2	96·6	94·8	66·1	97·5	94·0	124·7	97·4	71·9
1963	87·6	98·4	96·5	67·1	99·3	94·6	128·3	99·6	72·5
1964	90·1	100·5	98·7	70·6	102·2	96·3	131·6	103·0	73·3
1965	96·5	104·2	101·7	74·6	106·0	98·7	135·1	107·5	74·2
1966	100·2	107·8	104·9	80·0	110·5	101·5	140·8	112·7	75·8
1967	104·7	113·4	109·7	84·4	116·6	106·3	144·8	119·4	78·7
1968	112·7	121·9	118·6	92·1	126·2	116·0	154·5	128·9	87·9
1969	116·9	127·7	124·7	93·2	131·3	119·7	162·7	134·2	93·5
1970	122·0	133·3	130·6	100·9	136·7	123·5	169·5	140·2	96·8
1971	126								

13. **WAGES** (continued)

2. Monthly average for state-employed labour force (continued)

(*current* (*new*) *rubles*)

	Construction total	*Construction workers*	*Trade, public catering supply and procurements*	*Housing, communal, and services*	*Health and social insurance*	*Education and welfare*	*Science and scientific services*	*Credit and state insurance*	*Administration (state, economic, co-operative and social)*
1940	33·9	31·0	25·0	26·1	25·5	32·3	46·7	33·4	38·8
1945	41·3	36·1	26·9	31·0	39·4	47·2	64·2	51·2	50·4
1950	60·1	56·5	46·9	49·1	48·5	66·7	93·0	66·4	68·3
1955	74·2	70·0	52·3	52·3	52·1	70·3	102·8	70·0	79·6
1958	86·6	83·2	58·1	55·3	58·9	69·4	105·9	72·1	84·2
1960	91·7	88·7	58·6	57·6	58·9	69·9	104·2	70·3	85·6
1961	96·8	93·4	61·0	59·4	59·8	72·5	105·2	72·5	88·1
1962	99·3	95·9	63·6	61·0	60·8	73·8	108·1	76·8	90·1
1963	101·6	98·3	64·5	62·6	62·0	75·3	109·7	78·1	93·6
1964	106·0	103·0	65·7	64·5	65·3	78·5	112·0	79·0	95·8
1965	112·4	108·0	75·2	72·0	79·0	93·6	116·8	86·3	105·9
1966	116·7	112·3	79·7	75·7	80·8	95·5	119·9	89·6	111·8
1967	124·2	119·3	82·8	79·0	82·3	96·5	123·9	93·7	114·3
1968	131·2	127·3	90·6	88·1	90·2	102·8	129·3	103.5	118·1
1969	139·9	136·6	92·9	91·3	91·1	103·9	132·6	106·8	119·7
1970	149·9	148·5	95·1	94·5	92·0	105·8	136·8	111·4	122·2

Sources: *Nar. Khoz. 1965*, 567–8; *1967*, 657–8; *1968*, 555–6; *1969*, 539–40; *1970*, 519–20
Pravda (23 January 1972)
Strana Sovetov za 50 let, 227
Trud v SSSR (1968), 137, 138–9, 140, 145

14. EDUCATION

1. Numbers receiving education at beginning of academic year starting in given calendar year

(*thousands*)

	Higher	*Secondary specialised*	*Professional–technical*	*General (primary, seven-year and full secondary schools)*
1914	127·4[x]	54·3[x]	106[x]	7,896[x] 9,656[y]
1922	216·7	121·6		7366 (7322)*
1923	208·3	149·9		(7966)*
1924	169·5	164·6		(9201)*
1925	167·0	181·3		10,289 (10,219)*
1926	168·0	180·6		(10,730)*
1927	168·5	189·4	243	11,638 (11,466)*
1928	176·6	206·3		12,239 (12,068)*
1929	204·2	237·5		13,725
1930	287·9	586·8		17,891
1931	405·9	707·3		20,933
1932	504·4	723·7		21,397
1933	458·3	588·9		22,096
1934	527·3	671·5		23,745
1935	563·5	712·9		25,946
1936	542·0	768·9		28,136
1937	547·2	862·5		30,148
1938	602·9	951·9		32,268
1939	619·9	945·0		32,922
1940	811·7	974·8	717	35,528
1945	730·2	1007·7	945	26,808
1946	871·7	1174·5		29,738
1947	936·6	1231·6		30,476
1948	1032·1	1264·0		32,699
1949	1132·1	1309·2		34,540

[x] Pre-1939 boundaries [y] Present boundaries

* The figures in brackets exclude schools for working and rural youth, and adults.

14. EDUCATION (continued)

1. Numbers receiving education at beginning of academic year starting in given calendar year (continued)
(*thousands*)

	Higher	*Secondary specialised*	*Professional–technical*	*General (primary, seven-year and full secondary schools)*
1950	1247·4	1297·6	882	34,752
1951	1356·1	1368·9		34,037
1952	1441·5	1477·4	774	32,643
1953	1562·0	1645·5	1029	32,157
1954	1730·5	1838·7		31,486
1955	1867·0	1960·4	1356	30,070
1956	2001·0	2012·2	1365	30,127
1957	2099·1	1941·1	1392	30,623
1958	2178·9	1875·9	904	31,483
1959	2267·0	1907·8	996	33,364
1960	2396	2060	1113	36,187
1961	2640	2370	1266	39,087
1962	2944	2668	1397	42,445
1963	3261	2983	1491	44,682
1964	3608	3326	1607	46,664
1965	3861	3659	1672	48,255
1966	4123	3994	1961	48,170
1967	4311	4167	2129	48,902
1968	4470	4262	2263	49,195
1969	4550	4302	2348	49,426
1970	4581	4388	2411	49,373

Sources: *Dostizheniya Sovetskoi vlasti za 40 let v tsifrakh* (1957), 273
Kul'turnoe Stroitel'stvo SSSR (1956), 76, 80–1
Nar. Khoz. 1958, 806–7; *1962*, 551; *1964*, 667; *1968*, 669; *1969*, 665; *1970*, 627

14. **EDUCATION** (continued)

2. Output of specialists from higher and secondary specialised education

(*thousands*)

	Higher	*Secondary specialised*
1914	12·2	—
1928	28·7	28·6
1929	32·5	37·9
1930	43·9	61·4
1931	50·4	84·2
1932	43·2	107·7
1933	34·6	132·7
1934	49·2	97·3
1935	83·7	112·2
1936	97·6	124·9
1937	104·8	155·9
1938	103·8	201·2
1939	98·3	240·1
1940	126·1	236·8
1945	54·6	118·1
1946	76·0	180·1
1947	98·5	238·0
1948	138·0	277·3
1949	162·6	269·4
1950	176·9	313·7
1951	201·4	263·2
1952	219·2	280·6
1953	220·2	295·5
1954	234·8	332·3
1955	245·8	387·8
1956	259·9	510·1
1957	266·5	504·0
1958	290·8	551·2
1959	338·0	527·9
1960	343·3	483·5
1961	325·5	429·5
1962	316·6	452·2
1963	331·7	510·7
1964	354·0	558·3
1965	403·9	621·5
1966	431·8	685·2
1967	479·5	805·9
1968	510·6	902·8
1969	564·9	1019·2
1970	630·8	1033·3

Sources: *Nar. Khoz. 1962*, 569; *1964*, 686; *1968*, 688; *1969*, 684; *1970*, 645
Vysshee obrazovanie v SSSR (1961), 93, 239–40

14. EDUCATION (continued)

3. Numbers with higher and secondary specialised education in state-employed labour force
(*thousands*)

	Total	*Higher*	*Secondary specialised*
1913	190	136	54
1928	521	233	288
1941 (1:I)	2401	909	1492
1946 (1:I)	2262	897	1365
1950 (1:VII)	3254	1443	1811
1951 (1:VII)	3611	1576	2035
1952 (1:VII)	3951	1724	2227
1953 (1:VII)	4279	1848	2431
1954 (1:IV)	4638	2009	2629
1955 (1:VII)	5133	2184	2949
1956 (1:XII)	6257	2633	3624
1957 (1:XII)	6821	2805	4016
1958 (end of year, est.)	7476	3027	4449
1959 (1:XII)	8017	3236	4781
1960 (1:XII)	8784	3545	5239
1961 (1:XII)	9433	3824	5609
1962 (1:XII)	9956	4050	5906
1963 (1:XII)	10,484	4283	6201
1964 (15:XI)	11,250	4548	6702
1965 (15:XI)	12,066	4891	7175
1966 (15:XI)	12,924	5227	7697
1967 (end of year, est.)	13,855	5565	8290
1968 (15:XI)	14,956	6042	8914
1969 (end of year, est.)	16,100	6500	9600
1970 (16:XI)	16,841	6853	9988

Sources: *Nar. Khoz. 1969*, 549; *1970*, 523
Trud v SSSR (1968), 251

15. STATE BUDGET

1. Expenditure:

Single state budget—current data (*m. rubles*)

	Total	*Economy*	*Social and cultural*	*(Education)*	*(Health)*	*Defence and administration*
1923/24	2317·6	1151·9	133·1	113·6	13·9	647·5
1924/25	2969·5	1629·5	198·7	153·9	24·1	686·5
1925/26	4050·9	2244·6	275·9	227·7	34·3	899·6
1926/27	5334·6	3066·9	356·4	293·8	43·9	1002·4
1927/28	6465·0	3796·4	426·0	340·1	50·4	1109·3
1928/29	8240·9	4784·3	481·7	398·2	44·7	1206·9
1929/30	12,335·0	7680·7	794·9	704·6	49·0	1396·9
1930 (4th quarter)	4616·0	3124·7	295·8	275·8	12·2	533·4
1931	23,145·8	18,047·7	1290·7	1171·6	74·1	1714·5
1932	30,740·4	23,663·6	1705·8	1523·4	103·9	1987·3

Source: *Sots. stroi. SSSR* (1934), 442–3

Total budget—state and local (*m. rubles*)

	Total	*Economy*	*Social and cultural*	*(Education)*	*Defence and administration*	*Expenses of state loans*
1928/29	8023·8	4112·1	1495·9	1085·4	1588·1	317·5
1929/30	12,609·4	7087·4	2207·4	1678·4	1871·4	405·7
1930 (4th quarter)	4749·2	2800·4	742·3	607·8	680·5	74·9
1931	23,367·1	16,506·8	3373·8	2709·9	2398·2	408·3
1932	34,401·6	24,781·6	4577·4	3683·6	2838·3	961·8
1933	39,904·6	26,710·6	5840·0	4725·0	3370·8	1436·7
1934	52,398·0	32,257·1	8146·8	6161·0	8094·2	2050·9
1938	123,996	51,709	35,316	18,774	32,773	1955

Note. The two series above are not compatible, but neither is available for the full period.

The 'Social and cultural' heading includes 'Education' and 'Health' subheadings in all budget tables.

Sources: *Sots. Stroi. SSSR* (1936), 663
Sots. Stroi. Soyuza SSR 1933–38, 111 (for 1938 figures)

15. STATE BUDGET* (continued)

1. Expenditure (continued)

(million rubles—current prices)†

	Total	*National economy*	*Social and cultural*	*(Education and science)*	*(Health)*	*Defence*	*Administration*
1940	17·4	5·8	4·1	2·3	0·90	5·7	0·68
1950	41·3	15·8	11·7	5·7	2·1	8·3	1·4
1952	46·0	17·9	12·3	5·9	2·2	10·9	1·4
1953	51·5	18·1	12·9	6·1	2·4	10·8	1·4
1955	54·0	23·3	14·7	6·9	3·1	10·7	1·2
1956	56·4	24·5	16·4	7·4	3·6	9·7	1·2
1958	64·3	29·0	21·4	8·6	4·1	9·4	1·2
1959	70·4	32·4	23·1	9·4	4·5	9·4	1·1
1960	73·1	34·1	24·9	10·3	4·8	9·3	1·1
1961	76·3	32·6	27·2	11·3	4·9	11·6	1·1
1962	82·2	36·2	29·0	12·4	4·9	12·6	1·1
1963	87·0	38·8	31·0	13·7	5·2	13·9	1·1
1964	92·2	40·6	33·3	15·1	5·6	13·3	1·1
1965	101·6	44·9	38·2	17·5	6·7	12·8	1·3
1966	105·6	45·2	40·8	18·7	7·1	13·4	1·4
1967	115·2	52·8	43·5	20·1	7·5	14·5	1·5
1968	128·6	58·7	48·3	21·9	8·1	16·7	1·6
1969	138·5	62·4	51·9	23·3	8·6	17·7	1·7
1970	154·6	74·6	55·9	24·8	9·3	17·9	1·7

* 'State budget' includes central and local combined.
† New prices introduced in mid-1967.

Sources: *Gosudarstvennyi Byudzhet SSSR* (1966), 10–11, 20–1
Nar. Khoz. 1959, 800, 801; *1962*, 635; *1968*, 774; *1969*, 769; *1970*, 730

15. STATE BUDGET (continued)

2. Revenue: Single state budget—current data
(m. rubles)

	Total	*Turn-over tax*	*Indus-trial tax*	*Income tax*	*Agri-cultural tax*	*Excise duties*	*Non-tax revenue**	*State loans*
1923/24	2317·6	—	113·1	64·7	231·0	240·7	1039·2	183·5
1924/25	3002·2	—	157·3	94·3	326·2	507·8	1475·9	130·5
1925/26	4038·6	—	229·2	151·4	251·7	841·6	2095·7	146·0
1926/27	5375·3	—	348·9	192·2	357·9	1209·8	2558·8	319·2
1927/28	6614·4	—	373·4	231·4	354·2	1491·2	2922·3	726·4
1928/29	8222·3	—	1055·9	285·5	449·4	1802·6	3461·2	724·8
1929/30	12,799·7	—	1941·4	614·6	405·6	2643·0	5402·0	1278·4
1930 (4th quarter)	4670·7	2172·0	57·6	70·6	170·2	—	1742·4	356·1
1931	23,154·9	10,601·8	128·4	345·2	457·9	—	7381·8	3269·0
1932	31,030·9	17,693·4	—	245·2	459·0	—	7011·4	3921·7

* Includes deductions from profits, also revenue from transport and communications, state forests etc. There is a residual of miscellaneous other revenues—greater details of some categories are given in the sources.

Source: *Sots. stroi.* (1934), 440–1

Total budget—state and local (*m. rubles*)

	Total	*Turn-over tax*	*Deduc-tions from profits*	*Other non-tax**	*State loans†*	*Mass loans*	*Direct taxes*	*Social insur-ance*
1928/29	8116·1	3146·1	641·3	1206·1	454·6	270·2	979·4	—
1929/30	13,178·3	5354·1	1501·8	2061·7	622·4	656·0	972·1	—
1930 (4th) quarter)	4878·2	2172·0	464·9	771·5	143·6	212·4	396·5	—
1931	23,401·2	10,601·8	1631·2	3394·7	1644·4	1616·4	1704·1	—
1932	34,561·7	17,693·3	1657·4	4737·5	1492·4	2370·5	2699·2	—
1933	44,402·2	23,166·5	2071·9	6662·4	1211·5	3176·3	3309·6	—
1934	55,068·3	30,242·0	2375·3	8976·2	913·3	3343·7	3621·4	696·3
1938	127,571	80,411	10,598	—	—	5120	5047	—

* Transport, communications, and 'special commodity fund'.

† Classified in source as revenue from the socialised economy, in contrast to mass loans from the population.

Sources: *Sots. stroi.* (1936), 663
Sots. stroi. Soyuza SSR 1933–38, 111
(These two series are not compatible, like those given for budget expenditure; the series for revenue and expenditure for the same set of years are of course so.)

15. STATE BUDGET (continued)

2. Revenue (continued)

(mlrd rubles—current prices)*

	Total	*Turnover tax*	*Profits tax*	*Kolkhoz income tax*	*State loans†*	*Direct taxes*	*State social insurance*
1940	18·0	10·6	2·2	0·32	1·1	0·94	0·86
1950	42·3	23·6	4·0	0·55	3·1	3·6	1·9
1952	49·8	24·7	5·8	0·9	4·2	4·7	2·2
1953	54·0	24·4	7·0	0·95	3·0	4·6	2·3
1955	56·4	24·2	10·3	1·2	3·7	4·8	2·6
1956	58·6	25·9	10·3	1·4	4·4	5·1	2·8
1958	67·2	30·5	13·5	1·7	1·1	5·2	3·3
1959	74·0	31·1	16·0	1·9	1·5	5·5	3·6
1960	77·1	31·3	18·6	1·8	0·91	5·6	3·8
1961	78·1	30·9	20·7	1·2	0·80	5·8	4·2
1962	84·3	32·9	23·9	1·3	1·2	6·0	4·4
1963	89·5	34·5	25·7	1·4	1·3	6·3	4·6
1964	94·4	36·7	28·7	1·3	0·1	6·8	4·9
1965	102·3	38·7	30·9	1·5	0·2	7·7	5·6
1966	106·3	39·3	35·7	1·1	0·2	8·4	6·1
1967	117·2	40·1	41·8	1·3	0·1	9·3	6·5
1968	130·8	40·8	48·0	1·1	0·3	10·5	7·2
1969	140·0	44·5	48·0	1·1	0·4	11·6	7·9
1970	156·7	49·4	54·2	1·2	0·5	12·7	8·3

* New prices introduced in mid-1967.

† These are loans from the population, like pre-war 'mass-loans'.

Sources: *Gosudarstvennyi Byudzhet SSSR* (1966), 10–11, 20–1
Nar. Khoz. 1959, 800, 801; *1962*, 635; *1968*, 774; *1969*, 769; *1970*, 730

16. FOREIGN TRADE

1. Total exports and imports
*(m. rubles)**

	Old rubles at 1950 exchange rate		New rubles at 1961 exchange rate				
	Exports	Imports	Exports	Imports		Exports	Imports
1913	5298	4792			1945	301·8	259·7
1918	28	367	6·4	82·5	1946	588·3	692·0
1919	0·3	11	0·1	2·5	1947	693·7	670·3
1920	5	100	1·1	22·5	1948	1177·3	1101·6
1921	70	734	15·8	165·2	1949	1302·5	1340·3
1921/22†	221	945	49·8	212·6	1950	1615·2	1310·3
1922/23	467	518	105·0	116·5	1951	2061·7	1791·7
1923/24	1300	814	292·6	183·1	1952	2510·9	2255·5
1924/25	2014	2521	453·0	567·3	1953	2653·0	2492·1
1925/26	2451	2636	551·5	593·1	1954	2960·8	2863·6
1926/27	2812	2487	632·7	559·5	1955	3084·0	2754·5
1927/28	2759	3295	620·7	741·4	1956	3253·5	3251·4
1928 (Oct.-					1957	3943·3	3544·0
Dec.)	754	708	169·8	159·4	1958	3867·8	3914·6
1929	3219	3069	724·3	690·5	1959	4896·7	4565·9
1930	3612	3690	812·7	830·3	1960	5005·5	5065·6
1931	2827	3851	636·1	866·5	1961	5398·4	5244·9
1932	2004	2454	450·8	552·1	1962	6331·3	5804·8
1933	1727	1214	388·7	273·1	1963	6545·2	6352·9
1934	1458	810	328·0	182·3	1964	6913·2	6963·0
1935	1281	841	288·1	189·3	1965	7357·2	7252·5
1936	1082	1077	243·3	242·1	1966	7957·0	7121·6
1937	1312	1016	295·1	228·6	1967	8687·1	7683·0
1938	1021	1090	229·8	245·3	1968	9570·9	8469·0
1939	462	745	103·9	167·5	1969	10,489·7	9294·1
1940	1066	1091	239·7	245·5	1970	11,520·1	10,565·1
1941			178·5	277·7			
1942			65·7	181·8			
1943			66·8	173·1			
1944			114·9	198·8			

* Figures for war and post-war period in new (1961) rubles, converted at 1961 exchange rate. Figures for pre-war period in old rubles (10 old = 1 new) and converted at 1950 exchange rate. Total exports and imports for pre-war period are given in both forms, but all other pre-war foreign trade figures in old rubles at 1950 exchange rate only. Figures in new rubles at 1961 exchange rate are available for country totals for all pre-war years, but only for certain years for commodity structure.

† 1921/22 etc.: economic years during this period ran from 1 October.

16. FOREIGN TRADE (continued)

2. Trading Partners, 1913–40

(*m. rubles*)

	Austria		*Great Britain*		*Belgium and Luxemburg*		*Bulgaria*		*Hungary*		*Germany*	
	Exports	*Imports*	*Exports*	*Imports*	*Exports*	*Imports*	*Exports*	*Imports*	*Exports*	*Imports*	*Exports*	*Imports*
1913	227·6	124·4	933·3	603·0	225·4	31·0	8·17	0·112	—	—	1580·8	2276·2
1918	—	—	6·97	41·9	—	—	—	—	—	—	2·19	1·28
1919	—	0·028	—	0·094	—	—	—	—	—	—	—	0·899
1920	—	0·007	—	21·0	—	0·007	—	—	—	—	—	22·3
1921	—	8·88	32·6	215·2	—	2·41	—	0·003	—	—	5·81	189·5
1921/22	—	0·464	62·7	185·1	0·397	2·25	0·003	3·63	—	0·404	28·8	292·1
1922/23	0·310	1·40	100·8	129·7	5·90	2·69	1·05	0·045	1·83	—	150·9	214·2
1923/24	3·08	8·57	291·2	170·6	33·1	1·34	1·64	0·007	—	—	231·6	157·6
1924/25	10·4	37·9	673·6	385·8	67·2	11·6	1·18	0·122	0·146	2·13	304·5	357·8
1925/26	10·7	79·8	769·1	451·5	64·8	6·81	0·812	0·035	0·001	0·080	389·0	613·7
1926/27	12·5	69·4	768·6	352·3	48·1	0·572	0·530	0·070	—	1·01	611·7	563·2
1927/28	26·4	58·6	543·1	165·6	47·5	4·42	0·568	0·010	0·010	4·76	674·7	866·1
1928 (Oct.–Dec.)	6·40	12·3	163·3	23·4	11·1	5·68	0·480	—	0·080	0·592	183·5	169·3
1929	29·2	78·7	706·0	190·8	66·8	15·7	1·66	0·112	0·774	2·45	749·7	678·4
1930	12·4	51·7	975·5	279·3	93·8	22·9	0·254	0·042	0·028	0·972	716·9	874·2
1931	7·72	41·9	927·3	255·7	63·6	12·0	0·934	—	0·174	2·95	450·8	1431·1
1932	4·56	14·0	482·6	320·4	67·3	2·06	1·40	0·003	0·038	—	350·2	1142·1
1933	3·05	4·46	303·1	106·6	95·3	5·36	0·969	0·007	0·247	0·599	298·8	515·9
1934	1·42	5·40	241·1	109·2	60·1	25·2	0·464	0·003	0·749	1·20	343·0	100·2
1935	4·19	2·42	300·6	78·5	71·2	31·7	0·247	0·028	0·446	2·77	230·2	75·6
1936	0·915	2·65	287·8	76·7	70·2	32·7	0·195	—	0·599	0·268	92·8	245·4
1937	5·22	4·33	421·1	47·6	101·5	50·8	0·061	—	0·165	1·87	80·7	151·3
1938	1·69	3·43	283·0	131·7	88·2	48·5	0·308	—	0·078	—	64·8	50·7
1939	0·007	0·251	101·3	85·1	26·3	20·0	0·091	—	0·095	—	46·5	42·3
1940	—	—	0·416	10·0	0·464	8·7	20·1	18·7	2·93	—	555·9	316·3

16. FOREIGN TRADE (continued)

2. Trading Partners, 1913–40 (continued)

(m. rubles)

	Holland		*Italy*		*Poland*		*Rumania*		*Finland*		*France*	
	Exports	*Imports*	*Exports*	*Imports*	*Exports*	*Imports*	*Exports*	*Imports*	*Exports*	*Imports*	*Exports*	*Imports*
1913	618·3	74·5	257·1	58·6	—	—	75·6	4·89	192·7	177·6	351·6	198·6
1918	—	—	—	—	—	—	—	—	4·65	6·62	0·216	6·52
1919	—	—	—	—	—	0·010	—	—	—	0·150	—	0·098
1920	0·565	0·910	0·101	4·29	—	—	—	—	—	0·132	—	0·338
1921	0·547	9·69	0·017	0·279	0·083	1·42	—	0·001	0·007	14·6	—	27·3
1921/22	2·75	7·05	0·244	7·86	6·23	26·3	0·335	14·2	11·6	36·7	0·954	4·17
1922/23	24·9	8·25	11·7	2·58	10·9	31·3	1·28	0·001	17·9	19·9	2·03	0·568
1923/24	75·1	4·85	53·2	4·04	10·2	9·89	6·88	—	32·8	24·0	53·2	8·11
1924/25	71·5	119·9	53·8	18·28	13·1	35·8	1·84	—	8·74	65·0	77·1	32·1
1925/26	73·7	25·7	116·7	81·1	10·9	34·1	2·55	0·031	15·9	51·9	138·5	67·3
1926/27	81·2	17·6	131·2	11·5	67·9	46·4	2·85	—	36·5	62·4	188·5	77·4
1927/28	58·9	17·1	90·0	32·1	52·0	25·7	2·47	1·23	26·1	57·8	141·3	124·9
1928 (Oct.–Dec.)	23·7	2·48	30·0	7·1	10·8	12·5	0·017	0·003	3·16	10·6	42·6	21·2
1929	108·9	7·05	114·6	26·7	46·3	67·4	0·749	1·29	24·4	37·7	148·3	110·4
1930	121·4	16·4	185·2	37·6	49·2	135·1	3·00	0·038	13·0	43·3	153·9	103·5
1931	102·0	7·46	138·5	103·7	26·2	108·6	4·71	0·010	16·1	18·2	98·7	52·3
1932	75·0	12·4	94·2	94·6	16·7	19·7	4·63	0·003	18·6	10·1	100·0	15·1
1933	90·2	20·8	77·5	58·9	17·6	45·2	0·338	—	18·9	10·1	79·8	18·3
1934	77·5	27·7	66·3	41·2	12·7	18·3	0·495	0·0003	16·4	10·1	76·3	40·5
1935	55·7	54·2	44·9	19·7	11·7	9·12	0·610	0·010	12·3	4·81	62·9	61·2
1936	42·9	34·1	33·8	4·64	11·6	6·89	0·226	0·012	6·07	2·89	81·9	33·2
1937	84·4	22·0	12·5	2·30	9·85	3·37	2·18	1·37	7·06	2·89	65·9	20·9
1938	68·1	33·1	—	0·192	5·74	1·10	0·435	0·608	5·90	2·57	40·8	27·3
1939	15·4	29·0	10·9	0·112	5·56	1·00	0·079	—	6·65	2·76	21·4	11·1
1940	0·300	22·0	1·26	1·01	—	—	2·74	—	16·6	0·451	1·46	0·556

16. FOREIGN TRADE (continued)

2. Trading Partners, 1913–40 (continued)
(*m. rubles*)

	Czechoslovakia		*Yugoslavia*		*India*		*Iran*		*China*		*Mongolia*	
	Exports	*Imports*	*Exports*	*Imports*	*Exports*	*Imports*	*Exports*	*Imports*	*Exports*	*Imports*	*Exports*	*Imports*
1913	—	—	1·72	0·007	0·142	120·4	201·1	152·0	100·4	263·7	9·37	29·3
1918	—	—	—	—	—	—	—	—	—	20·5	—	—
1919	—	—	—	—	—	—	—	0·795	—	0·010	—	—
1920	—	—	—	—	—	—	0·140	0·627	—	—	—	—
1921	—	0·001	—	—	—	—	1·46	3·46	—	0·227	—	—
1921/22	0·195	5·66	—	—	—	0·031	4·99	3·23	—	0·237	—	—
1922/23	0·049	0·756	—	—	—	0·181	1·58	8·04	—	0·059	—	—
1923/24	0·659	9·24	2·43	—	—	1·74	26·0	77·5	16·3	38·9	5·25	6·86
1924/25	1·31	76·0	0·003	0·010	1·25	31·0	99·8	181·8	31·7	58·8	9·65	12·5
1925/26	1·78	65·7	0·007	0·001	—	46·2	122·4	153·1	60·0	108·1	12·8	13·0
1926/27	7·73	39·8	0·080	0·003	2·12	62·2	150·8	142·9	65·3	104·5	16·1	26·5
1927/28	13·1	60·6	0·003	0·453	14·6	89·3	252·4	218·2	85·3	157·8	26·7	42·2
1928 (Oct.–Dec.)	7·3	22·9	—	0·185	6·59	20·3	71·4	51·2	28·0	25·2	7·19	15·6
1929	29·2	64·2	0·457	1·18	17·8	98·3	242·6	211·4	81·4	120·4	35·0	53·2
1930	14·4	94·6	0·443	0·098	23·6	63·8	210·1	154·7	99·4	85·3	62·1	68·8
1931	17·9	124·5	0·118	0·007	35·4	31·9	113·2	161·9	87·2	59·7	130·1	100·5
1932	4·81	35·9	0·017	0·268	18·2	15·9	88·4	174·0	82·9	63·4	144·3	67·2
1933	3·82	17·0	0·115	0	11·9	10·3	41·8	29·1	62·8	74·8	134·4	60·2
1934	2·91	6·77	0·206	0·533	9·65	6·57	41·1	49·9	23·6	32·7	156·2	71·7
1935	4·56	20·6	0·645	0·003	10·5	17·1	54·6	72·1	22·9	28·2	40·5	27·6
1936	8·15	34·4	0·395	—	10·6	21·8	50·4	72·5	29·2	30·6	40·1	25·6
1937	12·5	10·3	0·550	1·08	6·57	20·3	69·2	64·0	26·7	30·7	49·7	25·4
1938	9·91	14·7	0·081	—	2·74	10·1	43·5	48·1	32·8	63·6	52·2	29·1
1939	2·67	11·0	0·040	1·93	1·62	5·94	1·23	2·61	25·7	78·7	56·9	37·3
1940	2·07	16·4	0·022	0·866	—	0·385	14·8	14·8	39·2	77·3	89·3	39·4

16. FOREIGN TRADE (continued)

2. Trading Partners, 1913–40 (continued)

(m. rubles)

	Malaya and Straits Settlements		*Japan*		*Canada*		*U.S.A.*		*Egypt*		*Australia*	
	Exports	*Imports*	*Exports*	*Imports*	*Exports*	*Imports*	*Exports*	*Imports*	*Exports*	*Imports*	*Exports*	*Imports*
1913	—	—	4·91	16·9	—	—	49·3	275·6	30·2	20·7	0·416	1·28
1918	—	—	—	—	—	—	2·59	50·0	—	—	—	—
1919	—	—	—	0·052	—	—	—	0·010	—	—	—	—
1920	—	—	—	—	—	—	—	3·41	—	—	—	—
1921	—	—	—	—	—	4·44	0·001	140·9	—	—	—	—
1921/22	—	—	—	0·003	—	4·60	0·010	153·3	—	—	—	0·031
1922/23	—	—	—	—	—	0·014	1·90	15·4	—	—	—	0·265
1923/24	—	—	51·5	8·85	—	0·422	25·0	177·7	7·12	0·551	—	7·11
1924/25	—	—	44·0	9·33	—	8·34	98·8	703·3	21·6	80·0	0·0003	104·1
1925/26	—	—	44·4	8·96	0·014	2·26	106·9	425·7	10·2	92·6	—	58·6
1926/27	—	—	66·9	12·6	0·237	8·89	81·7	508·4	20·5	72·5	0·001	54·3
1927/28	—	—	61·3	18·9	—	39·7	97·5	654·4	33·1	113·6	0·046	101·2
1928 (Oct.–Dec.)	—	5·06	11·4	4·54	—	2·07	30·9	103·7	6·2	35·1	—	34·0
1929	—	18·6	67·2	28·8	—	3·63	148·9	617·6	31·5	76·7	0·106	60·8
1930	—	23·1	55·8	58·5	4·07	4·97	142·6	921·4	31·6	64·2	0·965	42·4
1931	—	6·79	69·1	44·1	0·003	0·502	79·1	801·3	12·8	69·0	0·021	10·7
1932	—	5·69	35·2	16·7	3·52	7·17	59·9	110·4	21·5	3·30	0·265	20·4
1933	—	0·178	31·8	25·6	0·080	2·65	48·7	57·8	14·1	—	0·003	0·383
1934	—	32·7	20·1	24·1	0·816	5·06	49·8	62·3	10·8	—	0·001	6·23
1935	—	47·3	19·2	37·9	0·857	7·47	92·5	102·8	15·9	0·010	0·031	15·6
1936	—	57·4	22·0	49·3	0·623	2·58	103·5	166·3	11·2	—	0·041	19·9
1937	—	62·7	8·93	41·0	3·20	41·5	101·4	185·6	9·36	—	0·022	24·4
1938	—	41·5	5·27	11·9	1·17	23·1	67·1	308·4	9·05	0·211	0·005	38·4
1939	—	32·1	0·088	2·01	0·706	3·60	64·7	229·0	1·10	0·001	0·061	13·3
1940	—	8·2	0·969	3·65	—	1·18	85·5	338·4	0·675	—	0·045	—

16. FOREIGN TRADE (continued)

3. Trading Partners, 1946–
(*m. rubles*)

	E. Germany		*Poland*		*Czechoslovakia*		*Bulgaria*		*Hungary*		*Rumania*	
	Exports	*Imports*	*Exports*	*Imports*	*Exports*	*Imports*	*Exports*	*Imports*	*Exports*	*Imports*	*Exports*	*Imports*
1946	36·9	45·3	95·8	97·6	26·1	29·0	75·5	46·5	9·2	9·5	27·3	20·2
1947	39·3	19·6	94·0	123·4	39·9	35·1	56·2	34·4	14·6	15·5	33·9	24·6
1948	82·3	55·6	119·6	156·3	127·6	122·3	71·5	58·4	31·0	25·7	43·4	82·4
1949	104·5	131·7	123·2	167·8	185·4	184·5	84·6	49·7	75·3	60·2	100·2	89·6
1950	167·2	144·1	217·3	189·0	198·4	181·4	90·0	60·2	114·2	74·9	102·5	125·3
1951	268·8	295·1	279·6	237·7	261·1	227·8	104·3	66·6	109·6	102·7	128·6	125·3
1952	389·6	328·7	326·1	315·8	327·0	269·4	106·1	98·1	135·3	126·5	203·4	176·4
1953	454·6	435·0	296·0	330·6	313·9	281·1	98·6	112·2	141·9	155·1	198·7	206·7
1954	434·4	555·9	372·1	304·2	316·4	286·3	97·6	123·0	137·7	150·0	191·4	175·2
1955	430·8	455·8	388·6	258·0	320·3	347·9	114·7	109·3	103·8	131·8	241·0	188·8
1956	514·2	563·7	321·5	255·0	336·3	356·8	97·6	130·2	114·2	108·7	190·8	211·8
1957	775·9	687·9	387·8	230·3	496·2	347·0	155·2	178·3	224·7	96·1	225·7	171·0
1958	719·8	734·3	339·1	238·6	402·1	460·9	180·5	182·8	180·5	145·7	226·2	210·2
1959	927·1	800·5	437·8	284·9	542·7	523·7	260·9	234·7	233·8	185·9	209·2	224·5
1960	946·5	836·2	441·7	348·0	567·7	587·2	296·1	268·7	280·3	223·4	234·6	252·0
1961	1088·2	788·3	477·6	429·2	587·4	627·9	320·6	293·5	323·4	294·1	262·6	306·7
1962	1235·5	965·4	534·7	507·8	693·6	742·3	403·0	349·9	370·0	349·9	337·3	313·5
1963	1182·5	1173·3	596·3	553·1	764·1	855·5	445·9	400·3	399·1	380·8	359·1	369·2
1964	1246·5	1194·9	594·0	646·1	810·7	872·0	510·0	480·0	443·4	433·4	443·7	379·0
1965	1226·7	1156·2	654·0	702·6	833·3	931·9	529·6	554·0	491·3	463·8	362·5	396·9
1966	1266·1	1114·2	722·9	659·9	804·6	827·5	627·4	588·7	454·1	460·7	347·7	364·9
1967	1274·6	1271·4	821·0	812·2	870·7	884·0	686·5	696·4	527·0	537·4	355·1	381·9
1968	1355·8	1444·8	945·1	928·4	934·3	891·0	854·4	802·2	607·9	602·1	375·0	410·8
1969	1565·1	1466·4	1078·9	1011·8	998·7	1003·2	876·9	877·2	630·0	647·2	428·8	404·5
1970	1738·1	1556·9	1214·9	1134·9	1082·7	1110·5	844·0	972·5	758·3	721·6	444·6	474·0

3. Trading Partners, 1946 (continued)

(*m. rubles*)

	Mongolia		Cuba		China		N. Vietnam		N. Korea		Yugoslavia	
	Exports	Imports	Exports	Imports	Exports	Imports	Exports	Imports	Exports	Imports	Exports	Imports
1946	37·8	25·5	0	—	11·4	55·7	—	—	3·4	5·2	16·6	22·3
1947	40·7	33·5	0	0	68·9	72·2	—	—	12·4	9·1	33·9	26·6
1948	35·5	30·3	0	0	112·1	81·2	—	—	25·6	22·8	31·0	41·7
1949	38·5	32·4	0	—	179·7	128·9	—	—	82·6	57·0	2·6	9·6
1950	38·9	35·3	0	—	349·4	169·5	—	—	62·4	38·7	0	0
1951	71·4	50·6	0	—	430·6	298·2	—	—	16·4	26·8	0	0
1952	59·5	45·5	0	—	498·8	372·4	—	—	35·6	26·1	0	0
1953	78·6	45·1	—	0·8	627·8	427·2	—	—	29·5	23·1	0	—
1954	119·2	49·6	—	0·6	683·4	520·5	0	—	16·5	25·0	1·8	1·0
1955	109·5	48·4	—	32·2	673·5	579·2	3·3	0	39·7	36·7	14·8	15·7
1956	93·1	48·8	—	13·2	659·7	687·8	5·2	1·2	48·4	46·1	62·2	44·7
1957	60·9	45·1	—	42·4	489·7	664·3	8·7	2·9	54·0	56·3	65·8	51·1
1958	58·3	42·5	—	13·9	570·6	793·1	7·4	8·9	52·2	42·4	46·0	45·8
1959	70·8	44·6	0	6·7	859·1	990·3	17·9	14·0	66·7	46·4	41·6	47·8
1960	74·6	50·7	67·2	93·4	735·4	763·3	22·0	20·8	35·5	67·2	49·6	47·8
1961	83·2	52·4	258·3	280·7	330·6	496·3	37·2	23·1	69·3	71·2	32·3	49·1
1962	113·6	54·3	333·7	210·6	210·1	464·7	49·2	27·2	72·6	79·4	65·1	41·4
1963	102·6	46·5	359·8	148·0	168·5	371·7	51·0	31·8	73·9	79·3	86·7	78·3
1964	126·8	51·7	331·1	259·6	121·7	282·8	42·5	31·3	74·6	72·6	120·7	108·8
1965	114·1	55·7	337·9	308·0	172·5	203·0	67·4	27·5	80·8	79·5	130·6	169·8
1966	142·2	56·1	431·9	257·3	157·8	128·8	61·4	22·8	77·0	83·1	192·5	173·5
1967	167·8	55·9	506·7	335·5	45·3	51·0	132·9	18·8	99·3	97·2	252·5	209·3
1968	174·5	47·8	561·8	250·0	53·4	33·0	143·3	16·1	155·0	108·8	260·2	195·4
1969	176·6	47·5	561·6	208·5	25·0	26·1	170·4	15·2	181·4	113·9	220·3	205·0
1970	178·3	52·6	580·0	465·0	22·4	19·5	166·5	16·7	207·0	128·9	293·5	226·3

16. **FOREIGN TRADE** (continued)

3. Trading Partners, 1946 (continued)
(*m. rubles*)

	Great Britain		*France*		*Italy*		*W. Germany*		*Finland*		*Japan*	
	Exports	*Imports*	*Exports*	*Imports*	*Exports*	*Imports*	*Exports*	*Imports*	*Exports*	*Imports*	*Exports*	*Imports*
1946	28·0	7·7	34·2	0·7	0·4	0·1	—	—	30·2	31·8	0	0
1947	39·0	32·1	10·0	0·1	3·8	0·9	—	—	33·6	35·5	1·9	0·1
1948	123·2	24·1	7·2	0·2	2·7	4·2	—	—	56·9	52·0	5·1	2·4
1949	60·8	33·0	3·1	1·7	20·2	15·5	1·1	—	45·0	58·2	1·7	6·8
1950	92·0	36·2	2·9	3·6	14·6	19·1	0	—	27·9	27·0	3·6	0·6
1951	141·9	70·0	7·7	6·8	16·1	22·0	0	—	45·1	63·5	0	0
1952	117·3	111·5	8·0	9·5	30·3	23·8	0	0·1	92·4	109·0	0·3	0·2
1953	81·1	47·7	15·7	18·9	7·4	18·2	1·6	3·0	113·4	132·3	2·0	0
1954	99·6	46·5	41·0	32·4	34·7	26·4	10·4	9·5	95·2	137·6	1·8	0
1955	152·2	64·0	53·7	32·5	15·7	14·7	26·3	21·4	95·6	115·0	2·0	1·6
1956	133·3	67·0	62·7	45·5	30·5	23·4	37·6	61·3	103·3	131·6	2·7	0·7
1957	158·5	100·9	60·3	42·8	26·2	40·9	64·5	55·7	135·4	148·7	7·6	7·8
1958	131·0	65·6	78·4	72·5	34·7	31·7	59·1	64·9	105·4	123·5	17·9	16·0
1959	149·1	81·8	79·0	90·4	70·2	47·5	80·3	108·1	130·1	127·9	30·0	21·1
1960	173·2	97·3	66·4	116·9	92·4	81·3	106·9	179·3	134·3	129·8	68·5	55·4
1961	204·1	115·4	71·5	108·4	117·2	86·4	106·9	161·4	123·2	127·8	101·7	59·9
1962	191·8	104·8	76·9	137·7	118·3	88·7	121·0	183·9	161·8	194·1	101·7	131·2
1963	193·5	116·9	93·2	63·8	123·0	122·5	118·0	134·1	196·4	188·1	111·5	148·9
1964	214·7	92·9	95·3	62·3	121·0	88·5	112·4	177·6	198·5	151·1	148·2	173·9
1965	262·0	136·8	99·5	102·9	133·2	91·5	128·7	119·8	190·9	217·4	166·5	159·6
1966	297·0	152·0	117·1	144·3	139·6	85·9	166·9	125·4	231·4	195·3	214·8	201·8
1967	272·8	177·7	130·1	169·5	209·3	139·0	172·6	146·5	219·5	241·8	317·7	149·1
1968	330·0	245·7	123·5	264·9	208·9	187·6	189·3	204·6	219·6	239·3	352·1	166·5
1969	384·2	216·3	126·8	126·0	208·4	285·1	198·8	298·0	236·2	264·6	321·3	237·4
1970	418·2	223·2	290·6	286·8	190·4	281·4	223·4	320·6	258·3	272·4	341·4	310·9

16. FOREIGN TRADE (continued)

3. Trading Partners, 1946 (continued)
(*m. rubles*)

	U.S.A.		*Canada*		*Australia*		*India*		*U.A.R.*		*Malaysia*	
	Exports	*Imports*	*Exports*	*Imports*	*Exports*	*Imports*	*Exports*	*Imports*	*Exports*	*Imports*	*Exports*	*Imports*
1946	90·9	213·0	0·7	5·1	0	—	1·0	8·3	1·5	—	—	—
1947	70·7	99·3	0·2	0·1	0	0·3	2·9	4·7	3·3	—	—	12·0
1948	73·1	46·6	0·3	—	0	29·4	9·2	11·1	41·6	47·9	—	40·6
1949	43·7	22·7	0·1	0	0·7	23·8	36·5	12·1	3·5	35·9	—	28·2
1950	43·2	7·2	0·3	0	1·6	24·7	2·1	4·1	19·3	24·7	—	30·5
1951	23·8	0·5	0·8	—	1·7	13·4	11·2	11·0	21·8	6·1	—	18·5
1952	15·8	0·4	1·6	0	0·8	0	0·3	6·9	26·9	27·6	—	4·5
1953	14·8	0·4	0·7	0	1·9	19·6	0·9	0·8	11·3	10·8	—	3·7
1954	14·2	0·5	0·7	4·6	1·2	36·9	2·2	7·4	7·6	8·0	—	—
1955	21·4	0·5	1·8	2·3	1·1	6·1	6·6	4·0	9·9	13·8	—	19·6
1956	24·5	3·9	1·9	22·1	0	0	36·4	16·5	34·6	45·3	0·3	75·6
1957	14·4	9·1	3·8	8·0	0	0·4	76·2	37·8	74·0	99·8	0·6	43·9
1958	23·5	4·2	2·1	22·7	0·4	0	117·0	45·8	78·9	96·4	0	106·2
1959	23·1	16·0	3·6	13·6	0·2	5·1	61·2	54·5	79·2	83·4	0·8	114·0
1960	22·2	53·9	4·7	9·0	0·4	31·2	42·4	61·6	62·8	109·2	1·9	100·4
1961	21·9	45·6	4·2	41·1	0·6	26·0	85·9	60·2	97·8	86·6	1·8	152·6
1962	15·7	24·3	2·3	2·4	0·4	26·7	112·3	64·5	93·0	65·7	2·0	144·9
1963	22·3	25·1	3·1	157·3	1·1	52·5	199·7	85·3	121·7	111·2	3·9	120·4
1964	18·6	146·3	4·7	291·8	1·1	122·2	208·6	140·3	140·1	111·2	3·0	63·8
1965	31·0	58·2	12·2	227·8	1·4	90·7	193·5	169·4	187·8	147·1	0	101·4
1966	42·0	57·0	13·1	311·7	0·9	34·3	174·0	172·0	178·8	135·0	0	113·0
1967	35·4	56·3	20·3	126·7	1·3	17·3	146·2	162·7	253·2	130·6	0·1	86·9
1968	38·6	50·9	17·6	113·6	1·0	35·9	165·0	164·6	178·2	153·6	0·1	90·4
1969	54·5	105·1	10·5	29·6	1·7	40·2	154·2	199·3	214·4	205·3	1·5	109·6
1970	57·8	103·1	7·5	117·8	1·5	60·3	122·3	242·6	326·9	279·5	1·6	111·0

16. FOREIGN TRADE (continued)

4. Exports—some commodities

	Machinery and equipment (m. rubles)	(motor vehicles)* (units)	Oil (000 tons)	Rolled metal products (ferrous) (000 tons)	Copper (000 tons)	Round and sawn timber (000 tons)	Furs (m. rubles)	Grain (m. tons)
1913	13·8	—	952·5	27·5	0·350	7353·6	22·6	9·182
1918	0·073	—	1·72	0·076	2·062	2·94	4·79	0·002
1919	—	—	0·013	—	—	—	—	—
1920	—	—	0·085	—	—	0·484	0·007	0·004
1921	0·007	—	7·39	—	0·0004	156·8	9·76	0·003
1921/22	0·301	—	52·3	0·819	0·017	504·1	7·71	0·001
1922/23	0·923	—	84·3	0·068	0·0001	919·0	17·7	0·728
1923/24	1·31	—	711·6	4·05	0·027	2009·1	64·6	2·576
1924/25	5·68	—	1372·5	4·46	0·012	2086·6	234·6	0·569
1925/26	3·53	—	1473·5	2·74	0·015	1872·5	241·5	2·016
1926/27	2·48	—	2086·1	25·1	1·719	2429·1	300·1	2·099
1927/28	3·20	—	2782·8	7·32	0·076	2912·9	415·9	0·289
1928 (Oct.–Dec.)	0·279	—	795·9	5·24	0·006	1098·1	60·9	0·001
1929	2·81	—	3858·6	17·7	0·005	5376·6	371·6	0·178
1930	8·32	—	4713·0	13·7	0·043	7229·8	267·8	4·764
1931	16·4	—	5225·5	9·06	0·008	5914·6	195·9	5·056
1932	17·5	—	6117·7	8·04	0·013	5546·1	147·4	1·727
1933	16·3	—	4930·1	37·0	0·045	6115·7	134·4	1·684
1934	21·6	266	4315·2	22·7	0·002	6323·5	111·4	0·769
1935	27·3	844	3368·6	27·7	0·0004	6605·8	104·5	1·517
1936	23·4	1848	2665·6	46·5	0·001	5888·4	123·3	0·321
1937	41·8	3429	1929·3	81·0	0·001	4994·3	115·4	1·277
1938	51·2	6776	1388·4	53·0	0·001	3151·7	96·1	2·054
1939	14·6	618	474·2	9·5	0·002	1715·6	81·4	0·277
1940	21·1	1305	874·3	32·1	0·028	1006·9	82·3	1·155

* Motor vehicles are included in 'Machinery and equipment'.

	Machinery and equipment (m. rubles)	(Motor vehicles) (000)	Oil and oil products (m. tons)	Rolled metal products (ferrous) (m. tons)	Copper (000 tons)	Aluminium (000 tons)	Round and sawn timber† (m. cubic metres)	Cotton (000 tons)	Furs (m. rubles)	Grain (m. tons)	Refined sugar (m. tons)
1946	34	1·9	0·5	0·1	2·3	0·6	0·3	101·8	65·8	1·7	28·2
1947	20	3·2	0·8	0·1	3·7	0·9	0·5	138·4	44·1	0·8	17·8
1948	53	7·8	0·7	0·4	8·4	4·4	0·8	184·3	48·1	3·2	14·6
1949	119	11·8	0·9	0·6	16·9	9·9	1·4	191·6	35·8	2·4	62·8
1950	191	17·4	1·1	0·6	26·7	11·7	1·7	215·8	37·4	2·9	96·5
1951	306	16·2	2·5	0·8	36·0	20·0	1·4	235·2	35·7	4·1	124·4
1952	408	26·4	3·1	0·9	47·8	20·0	1·2	253·1	30·1	4·5	138·1
1953	471	27·0	4·2	1·2	44·5	40·6	1·9	269·8	24·8	3·1	195·2
1954	479	34·7	6·5	1·8	45·3	51·4	2·7	347·6	26·2	3·9	207·5
1955	539	35·3	8·0	1·51	36·7	41·6	3·9	336·9	34·8	3·7	209·7
1956	562	31·5	10·1	1·83	52·4	59·9	3·8	309·5	34·9	3·2	174·4
1957	587	34·2	13·7	1·92	60·6	85·4	5·8	318·7	33·9	7·4	190·5
1958	715	51·5	18·1	2·16	43·8	114·9	6·6	310·9	32·0	5·1	200·4
1959	1051	59·3	25·4	2·44	58·8	77·4	7·9	344·5	37·5	7·0	197·2
1960	1027	54·4	33·2	2·7	64·4	68·0	9·4	390·9	41·6	6·8	242·9
1961	868	51·8	41·2	3·02	60·4	86·0	10·9	382·6	39·2	7·480	413·7
1962	1052	61·0	45·4	3·53	71·3	115·7	13·4	343·6	44·2	7·814	792·4
1963	1292	58·3	51·4	3·54	72·0	122·1	14·6	321·5	62·9	6·259	802·4
1964	1450	65·7	56·6	4·18	89·5	175·2	17·1	393·6	53·0	3·513	347·7
1965	1472	63·7	64·4	4·55	93·1	229·0	19·1	457·7	52·1	4·330	604·1
1966	1654	96·2	73·6	5·02	120·1	255·7	20·7	507·8	60·1	3·556	992·8
1967	1832	102·7	79·0	5·16	94·0	253·1	19·8	534·4	52·0	6·248	1032·3
1968	2072	111·4	86·2	5·47	109·3	287·6	20·7	554·4	51·6	5·406	1299·6
1969	2361	106·4	90·8	6·5	107·4	320·0	21·5	452·3	47·5	7·2	1100
1970	2482	120·1	95·8	7·0	123·1	368·9	23·3	516·5	44·7	5·7	1100

* Motor vehicles are included in 'Machinery and equipment'.
† Pre-war timber figures are given in 000 tons, post-war figures in 000,000 cubic metres.

16. FOREIGN TRADE (continued)

5. Imports—some commodities

	Machinery and equipment (m. rubles)	Pipes (000 tons)	Copper (000 tons)	Natural rubber (000 tons)	Cotton (000 tons)	Wool (000 tons)	Grain† (000 tons)	Meat (000 tons)	Raw sugar (000 tons)	Clothing (m. rubles)	Leather footwear* (m. rubles)
1913	796·8	13·1	6·16	12·8	197·2	55·5	465·6	14·7	0·235	56·7	7·39
1918	18·2	—	—	0·512	1·98	0·385	—	—	—	0·836	18·3
1919	0·131	—	—	—	—	—	0·085	0·178	2·57	0·021	0·021
1920	15·1	0·178	—	—	0·0003	0·131	—	0·024	0·002	17·5	8·49
1921	93·7	7·34	—	0·429	0·483	0·054	141·9	9·70	6·94	57·7	179·1
1921/22	203·4	5·28	—	0·393	0·065	0·016	582·9	16·2	42·3	70·3	52·5
1922/23	110·9	5·50	—	0·131	29·9	1·47	13·4	7·09	21·5	12·0	4·16
1923/24	108·1	7·79	0·550	0·050	100·3	14·5	41·3	5·63	25·9	1·23	1·14
1924/25	344·3	5·59	1·52	4·89	107·1	17·8	281·3	0·281	227·8	1·61	0·739
1925/26	542·1	14·8	10·9	7·26	103·2	21·6	31·8	0·077	38·1	9·03	1·04
1926/27	547·2	30·1	18·2	11·0	162·7	29·8	43·6	0·185	4·27	2·16	0·390
1927/28	788·0	73·2	27·6	14·7	145·2	34·7	277·0	0·201	3·66	3·97	0·572
1928 (Oct.–Dec.)	172·1	24·2	3·64	2·23	27·9	11·8	1·04	0·017	0·001	1·87	0·028
1929	923·3	17·3	25·1	12·8	115·0	39·2	45·7	0·283	36·4	6·99	0·074
1930	1726·6	39·6	20·6	16·4	57·9	32·7	48·2	1·35	310·9	3·33	0·171
1931	2076·2	114·3	25·1	28·2	53·7	30·7	37·1	1·97	0·072	0·614	0·606
1932	1366·9	59·7	12·0	30·7	24·3	25·9	184·8	9·34	41·5	0·944	1·00
1933	521·9	90·2	7·87	31·3	22·6	28·5	12·8	6·09	6·94	3·60	0·662
1934	202·9	60·1	11·5	48·1	24·9	26·8	32·7	9·59	11·4	2·93	0·432
1935	198·1	38·8	29·6	38·3	44·2	34·3	15·3	5·99	0·256	1·26	0·358
1936	419·4	36·8	45·3	31·5	16·7	28·2	6·34	2·86	0·307	0·816	0·149
1937	278·5	29·1	65·3	31·0	22·1	31·1	0·060	2·87	0·177	0·420	0·171
1938	376·4	24·1	82·2	27·3	16·5	31·0	128·7	2·69	0·072	0·483	0·071
1939	288·3	2·55	35·7	30·7	3·99	24·9	154·5	2·43	0·010	0·318	0·068
1940	353·6	41·7	70·0	18·2	9·83	23·4	85·8	5·57	25·3	—	—

5. Imports—some commodities (continued)

	Machinery and equipment (m rubles)	Pipes (000 tons)	Copper (000 tons)	Natural rubber (000 tons)	Cotton (000 tons)	Wool (000 tons)	Grain (000 tons)	Meat (000 tons)	Raw sugar (000 tons)	Clothing (m. rubles)	Leather footwear (m. pairs)
1946	197	71·9	8·3	3·3	—	24·1	118·7	19·0	—	5·7	0·9
1947	119	51·0	1·8	43·2	—	27·4	254·5	12·1	—	7·1	1·1
1948	99	93·1	7·2	108·4	106·1	45·7	587·3	7·3	—	10·8	4·9
1949	193	102·7	4·1	86·9	85·3	36·3	134·2	17·3	—	14·6	7·4
1950	282	143·3	6·4	87·2	45·0	34·9	206·8	47·4	—	1·1	6·6
1951	372	164·5	1·5	127·2	4·1	32·2	239·7	50·9	—	8·3	3·5
1952	486	194·7	7·1	148·0	34·4	29·2	224·3	82·3	—	11·2	3·2
1953	685	206·6	13·2	70·0	20·3	41·4	86·0	126·5	9·6	9·8	1·8
1954	875	136·2	29·5	20·6	15·9	57·2	221·9	296·9	9·5	19·9	1·6
1955	833	123·1	43·8	35·3	19·9	46·5	305·6	240·8	205·6	20·3	0·9
1956	806	145·1	44·7	140·7	51·4	48·5	493·6	207·3	214·3	84·5	11·4
1957	846	122·6	59·3	145·5	108·8	57·3	152·5	116·8	350·9	135·5	11·8
1958	958	157·6	93·8	258·7	142·1	55·2	781·6	156·6	197·9	199·3	24·5
1959	1217	500·8	115·7	242·1	190·3	57·8	256·5	112·8	132·5	338·1	26·1
1960	1508	578·5	106·0	190·9	193·1	61·5	240·4	66·9	1467·8	360·0	29·7
1961	1561	631·0	82·2	360·3	141·6	55·3	678·7	59·7	3345·0	357·7	25·1
1962	2016	961·7	106·4	361·7	150·2	48·6	46·2	149·1	2233·2	398·7	25·2
1963	2219	656·6	88·0	298·4	225·6	42·4	3102·9	37·4	996·4	464·4	25·6
1964	2398	514·1	9·5	186·1	144·9	46·3	7286·5	119·9	1859·3	418·2	25·1
1965	2423	766·8	0·7	271·2	182·9	52·8	6375·2	252·2	2330·7	387·9	27·9
1966	2308	596·2	7·4	311·1	172·7	61·3	7746·4	133·2	1840·9	453·3	33·7
1967	2625	582·7	1·4	278·5	144·5	49·8	2187·4	57·5	2479·7	573·1	49·6
1968	3127	765·5	9·4	325·9	136·8	70·8	1605·9	59·6	1752·2	619·8	55·4
1969	3486	1000	0·405	295·0	170·5	75·8	639·1	75·8	1300	613·6	57·0
1970	3706	1300	1·021	316·5	257·7	82·7	2158·5	164·9	3200	699·2	60·7

Sources: *Vneshnyaya Torgovlya SSSR* 1918–40; 1918–1966; 1955–59; 1959–63; 1964; 1966; 1968; 1970

II. INDUSTRIAL PRODUCTION

17. COAL

(m. tons)

1913	29·1[x]
	29·2[y]
1917	31·3
1918	13·1
1919	9·4
1920	8·7
1921	9·5
1922	11·3
1923	12·7
1924	16·3
1925	16·5
1926	25·8
1927	32·3
1928	35·5
1929	40·1
1930	47·8
1931	56·8
1932	64·4
1933	76·3
1934	94·2
1935	109·6
1936	126·8
1937	128·0
1938	133·3
1939	146·2
1940	165·9
1945	149·3
1946	164·1
1947	183·2
1948	208·2
1949	235·5
1950	261·1
1951	281·9
1952	300·9
1953	320·4
1954	347·1
1955	391·3
1956	429·2
1957	463·5
1958	496·1
1959	506·6
1960	509·6
1961	506·4
1962	517·4
1963	531·7
1964	554·0
1965	577·7
1966	585·6
1967	595·2
1968	594·2
1969	607·8
1970	624·1
1971	641

[x] Pre-1939 territory
[y] Present territory
} These symbols recur frequently throughout for 1913 figures, with the same meaning.

Sources: *Nar. Khoz. 1968*, 238; *1969*, 201; *1970*, 187
Pravda (23 January 1972)
Promyshlennost' SSSR (1957), 140

18. OIL

(*m. tons*)

1913	9·2[x]	1945	19·4
	10·3[y]	1946	21·7
1914	9·2	1947	26·0
1915	9·4	1948	29·2
1916	10·0	1949	33·4
1917	8·8	1950	37·9
1918	4·1	1951	42·3
1919	4·4	1952	47·3
1920	3·9	1953	52·8
1921	3·8	1954	59·3
1922	4·7	1955	70·8
1923	5·3	1956	83·8
1924	6·1	1957	93·3
1925	7·1	1958	113·2
1926	8·3	1959	129·6
1927	10·3	1960	147·9
1928	11·6	1961	166·1
1929	13·7	1962	186·2
1930	18·5	1963	206·1
1931	22·4	1964	223·6
1932	21·4	1965	242·9
1933	21·5	1966	265·1
1934	24·2	1967	288·1
1935	25·2	1968	309·2
1936	27·4	1969	328·3
1937	28·5	1970	352·6
1938	30·2	1971	372
1939	30·3		
1940	31·1		

Sources: *Nar. Khoz. 1969*, 197; *1970*, 184
Pravda (23 January 1972)
Promyshlennost' SSSR (1956), 153; (1964), 205

19. NATURAL GAS

(*mlrd cubic metres*)

1913	—	1955	8·981
1928	0·304	1956	12·07
1932	1·049	1957	18·58
1937	2·179	1958	28·09
1940	3·219	1959	35·39
1945	3·278	1960	45·36
1950	5·761	1961	58·98
1951	6·252	1962	73·53
1952	6·384	1963	89·83
1953	6·869	1964	108·6
1954	7·512	1965	127·7
		1966	143·0
		1967	157·4
		1968	169·1
		1969	181·1
		1970	197·9
		1971	212*

* Includes approximately 2 mlrd cubic metres of gas from coal and shale.

Sources: *Nar. Khoz. 1969*, 199; *1970*, 185
Pravda (23 January 1972)
Promyshlennost' SSSR (1964), 213

20. ELECTRICITY

	All power stations		of which, hydro stations	
	Capacity (*m.*KW)	Output (*mlrd* KWH)	Capacity (*m.*KW)	Output (*mlrd* KWH)
1913	1·098[x] 1·141[y]	1·945[x] 2·039[y]	0·016	0·035
1916	1·192	2·575	0·016	0·037
1920		0·2		
1921	1·228	0·520	0·018	0·010
1922	1·247	0·776	0·019	0·012
1923	1·279	1·146	0·021	0·020
1924	1·308	1·562	0·023	0·030
1925	1·397	2·925	0·026	0·040
1926	1·586	3·508	0·089	0·050
1927	1·698	4·205	0·103	0·256
1928	1·905	5·007	0·121	0·430
1929	2·296	6·224	0·126	0·462
1930	2·875	8·368	0·128	0·555
1931	3·972	10·686	0·130	0·592
1932	4·677	13·540	0·504	0·812
1933	5·583	16·357	0·740	1·250
1934	6·315	21·011	0·840	2·376
1935	6·923	26·288	0·896	3·676
1936	7·529	32·837	0·956	4·013
1937	8·235	36·173	1·044	4·184
1938	8·941	39·366	1·173	5·084
1939	9·894	43·203	1·295	4·705
1940	11·193	48·309	1·587	5·113
1945	11·124	43·257	1·252	4·841
1946	12·338	48·571	1·427	6·046
1947	13·677	56·491	1·857	7·283
1948	15·157	66·341	2·191	9·369
1949	17·149	78·257	2·798	11·512

20. ELECTRICITY (continued)

	All power stations Capacity (*m.*KW)	Output (*mlrd* KWH)	*of which, hydro stations* Capacity (*m.*KW)	Output (*mlrd* KWH)
1950	19·614	91·226	3·218	12·691
1951	22·117	104·022	3·338	13·722
1952	25·250	119·116	3·814	14·908
1953	28·602	134·325	4·520	19·201
1954	32·815	150·695	5·135	18·561
1955	37·246	170·225	5·996	23·165
1956	43·470	191·653	8·498	28·984
1957	48·397	209·688	10·040	39·429
1958	53·641	235·350	10·863	46·478
1959	59·267	265·112	12·710	47·630
1960	66·721	292·274	14·781	50·913
1961	74·098	327·611	16·366	59·122
1962	82·461	369·275	18·622	71·944
1963	93·050	412·418	20·830	75·859
1964	103·584	458·902	21·251	77·361
1965	115·033	506·672	22·244	81·434
1966	123·007	544·566	23·077	91·823
1967	131·727	587·699	24·813	88·571
1968	142·504	638·661	27·035	104·040
1969	153·790	689·050	29·645	115·181
1970	166·750	740·400	31·368	124·377
1971		800		

Sources: *Nar. Khoz. 1969*, p. 192; *1970*, 179
Pravda (23 January 1972)
Promyshlennost' SSSR (1964), 231–2
SSSR i Zarubezhnye strany: stat. sbor. (1970), 50

21. IRON ORE

(*m. tons*)

1913	9·2[xy]	1945	15·9
1917	5·3	1946	19·3
1918	0·6	1947	23·3
1919	0·09	1948	28·0
		1949	32·6
1920	0·16	1950	39·7
1921	0·129	1951	44·9
1922	0·245	1952	52·6
1923	0·505	1953	59·7
1924	1·1	1954	64·3
1925	2·2	1955	71·9
1926	3·5	1956	78·1
1927	5·0	1957	84·3
1928	6·1	1958	88·8
1929	8·0	1959	94·4
1930	10·7	1960	105·9
1931	10·6	1961	117·6
1932	12·1	1962	128·1
1933	14·5	1963	137·5
1934	21·5	1964	145·9
1935	26·8	1965	153·4
1936	27·8	1966	160·3
1937	27·8	1967	168·2
1938	26·6	1968	176·6
1939	26·9	1969	186·1
1940	29·9	1970	195·5
		1971	203

Sources: *Nar. Khoz. 1932*, 6–7; *1959*, 169; *1969*, 207; *1970*, 193
Pravda (23 January 1972)
SSSR i Zarubezhnye strany: stat. sbor. (1970), 50

22. PIG IRON

(*m. tons*)

1913	4·2[xy]	1945	8·8
1917	3·0	1946	9·9
1918	0·60	1947	11·2
1919	0·12	1948	13·7
1920	0·12	1949	16·4
1921	0·12	1950	19·2
1922	0·18	1951	21·9
1923	0·31	1952	25·1
1924	0·67	1953	27·4
1925	1·3	1954	30·0
1926	2·2	1955	33·3
1927	3·0	1956	35·8
1928	3·3	1957	37·0
1929	4·0	1958	39·6
1930	5·0	1959	43·0
1931	4·9	1960	46·8
1932	6·2	1961	50·9
1933	7·1	1962	55·3
1934	10·4	1963	58·7
1935	12·5	1964	62·4
1936	14·4	1965	66·2
1937	14·5	1966	70·3
1938	14·7	1967	74·8
1939	14·5	1968	78·8
1940	14·9	1969	81·6
		1970	85·9
		1971	89·3

Sources: *Nar. Khoz. 1959*, 163; *1969*, 204; *1970*, 190
Pravda (23 January 1972)

23. STEEL

(m. tons)

1913	4·3[y]	1945	12·3
	4·2[x]	1946	13·3
		1947	14·5
1917	3·1	1948	18·6
1918	0·40	1949	23·3
1919	0·20		
1920	0·19	1950	27·3
1921	0·22	1951	31·4
1922	0·32	1952	34·5
1923	0·62	1953	38·1
1924	1·0	1954	41·4
1925	1·9	1955	45·3
1926	2·9	1956	48·7
1927	3·6	1957	51·2
1928	4·3	1958	54·9
1929	4·9	1959	60·0
1930	5·8	1960	65·3
1931	5·6	1961	70·8
1932	5·9	1962	76·3
1933	6·9	1963	80·2
1934	9·7	1964	85·0
1935	12·6	1965	91·0
1936	16·4	1966	96·9
1937	17·7	1967	102·2
1938	18·1	1968	106·5
1939	17·6	1969	110·3
1940	18·3	1970	115·9
		1971	121

Sources: *Nar. Khoz. 1959*, 163; *1969*, 204; *1970*, 190
Pravda (23 January 1972)

24. ROLLED STEEL PRODUCTS

(*m. tons*)

	Total	Finished rolled steel
1913	3·5	3·3[x]
		3·4[y]
1917	2·4	2·3
1918	0·36	
1919	0·18	
1920	0·15	
1921	0·17	0·15
1922	0·26	
1923	0·47	
1924	0·69	
1925	1·4	
1926	2·3	
1927	2·8	
1928	3·4	3·2
1929	3·9	
1930	4·6	
1931	4·3	
1932	4·4	4·1
1933	5·1	
1934	7·0	
1935	9·4	
1936	12·5	
1937	13·0	11·1
1938	13·3	
1939	12·7	
1940	13·1	11·4

	Total	Finished rolled steel
1945	8·5	7·4
1946	9·6	8·3
1947	11·1	
1948	14·2	
1949	18·0	
1950	20·9	18·0
1951	24·0	
1952	26·8	23·1
1953	29·4	25·4
1954	32·1	
1955	35·3	30·6
1956	37·8	32·4
1957	40·2	33·9
1958	43·1	36·3
1959	47·0	39·6
1960	51·0	43·7
1961	55·3	47·5
1962	59·3	51·4
1963	62·5	54·1
1964	66·7	57·4
1965	70·9	61·7
1966	76·7	66·1
1967	81·7	70·6
1968	85·3	74·1
1969	87·5	76·3
1970	92·4	80·6
1971	95·8	84·0

Sources: *Nar. Khoz. 1959*, 163, 166; *1962*, 149; *1963*, 145; *1964*, 169, 171; *1967*, 245; *1969*, 206; *1970*, 192
Pravda (23 January 1972)
Promyshlennost' SSSR (1964), 168–9

25. STEEL PIPES

(000 tons)

Year	Output	Year	Output
1913	77·7	1945	571
1917	56·3	1946	796
1918	8·2	1947	950
1919	4·1	1948	1324
1920	. .	1949	1728
1921	. .	1950	2001
1922	10·5	1951	2286
1923	27·8	1952	2616
1924	49·1	1953	3026
1925	75·3	1954	3339
1926	113	1955	3549
1927	132	1956	3851
1928	171	1957	4198
1929	189	1958	4623
1930	233	1959	5215
1931	284	1960	5805
1932	310	1961	6357
1933	348	1962	6878
1934	470	1963	7521
1935	639	1964	8124
1936	859	1965	9014
1937	923	1966	9905
1938	909	1967	10,582
1939	917	1968	11,215
1940	966	1969	11,551
		1970	12,434
		1971	13,400

Sources: *Nar. Khoz. 1959*, 163; *1969*, 204; *1970*, 192
Pravda (23 January 1972)

26. MINERAL FERTILISERS

(*m. tons, standard units*)

Year		Year	
1913	0·069[x]	1945	1·1
	0·089[y]	1946	1·7
1928	0·135	1947	2·4
1929	0·208	1948	3·5
1930	0·503	1949	4·6
1931	0·701	1950	5·5
1932	0·920	1951	5·9
1933	1·0	1952	6·4
1934	1·4	1953	7·0
1935	2·3	1954	8·1
1936	2·8	1955	9·7
1937	3·2	1956	10·9
1938	3·4	1957	11·8
1939	3·6	1958	12·4
1940	3·2	1959	12·9
		1960	13·9
		1961	15·3
		1962	17·3
		1963	19·9
		1964	25·5
		1965	31·3
		1966	35·9
		1967	40·1
		1968	43·5
		1969	45·9
		1970	55·4
		1971	61·4

Sources: *Nar. Khoz. 1959*, 202; *1969*, 212; *1970*, 198
Pravda (23 January 1972)

27. SULPHURIC ACID (MONOHYDRATE)

(*m. tons*)

Year	Output
1913	0·15[y]
	0·12[x]
1928	0·211
1929	0·265
1930	0·396
1931	0·464
1932	0·552
1933	0·627
1934	0·782
1935	0·994
1936	1·20
1937	1·37
1938	1·54
1939	1·63
1940	1·59
1945	0·781
1946	0·725
1947	0·996
1948	1·48
1949	1·85
1950	2·13
1951	2·37
1952	2·66
1953	2·92
1954	3·29
1955	3·80
1956	4·32
1957	4·57
1958	4·80
1959	5·08
1960	5·40
1961	5·72
1962	6·13
1963	6·89
1964	7·65
1965	8·52
1966	9·37
1967	9·74
1968	10·16
1969	10·67
1970	12·06
1971	12·78

Sources: *Nar. Khoz. 1959*, 204; *1969*, 211; *1970*, 197
Pravda (23 January 1972)
Promyshlennost' SSSR (1957), 196

28. PLASTICS AND SYNTHETIC RESINS

(000 tons)

	*post-1964 definition**	*pre-1964 definition**
1931	3·5	
1932	3·9	
1933	4·2	
1934	5·6	
1935	7·6	
1940	10·9	14·9
1945	21·3	27·0
1946	26·3	
1950	67·1	74·5
1951		73·3
1952		84·4
1953		103·6
1954		135·4
1955	160·3	177·3
1956		206·3
1957		225·2
1958	237·0	257·5
1959	271·6	292·7
1960	311·6	331·7
1961	383·7	404·4
1962	451·7	473·1
1963	567·2	589·4
1964	700·8	
1965	803·1	
1966	971·2	
1967	1113·6	
1968	1291·6	
1969	1452·6	
1970	1672	
1971	1862	

* From 1964 onwards a different definition, giving slightly lower figures, has been used. No post-1964 figures are available on the old definition, and only certain pre-1964 ones on the new definition. Hence the two series are given side by side. It is not clear whether the few figures available for the pre-war period are on the same definition as post-war before 1964.

Sources: *Nar. Khoz. 1965*, 190; *1969*, 214; *1970*, 200
Pravda (23 January 1972)
Promyshlennost' SSSR (1964), 146
Sots. stroi SSSR (1936), 177

29. CHEMICAL FIBRES

(000 tons)

1928	0·2	1955	110·5
1932	2·8	1956	128·9
1937	8·6	1957	148·7
1940	11·1	1958	166·0
1945	1·1	1959	179·4
1946	3·2	1960	211·2
1947	6·7	1961	250·4
1948	11·1	1962	277·3
1949	17·0	1963	308·4
1950	24·2	1964	361·1
1951	35·4	1965	407·3
1952	49·2	1966	458·3
1953	62·3	1967	510·6
1954	78·8	1968	553·7
		1969	583·5
		1970	623·0
		1971	676

Sources: *Nar. Khoz. 1959*, 205; *1969*, 214; *1970*, 200
Pravda (23 January 1972)
Promyshlennost' SSSR (1964), 148–9

30. TYRES*

(m. units)

1928	0·085	1950	7·40
1929	0·148	1951	7·52
		1952	7·60
1930	0·368	1953	8·11
1931	0·573	1954	9·28
1932	0·553		
1933	0·679	1955	10·2
1934	1·55	1956	11·3
		1957	12·8
1935	2·08	1958	14·4
1936	2·21	1959	15·5
1937	2·70		
1938	3·60	1960	17·2
1939	4·22	1961	19·0
		1962	20·8
1940	3·0	1963	22·6
1945	1·4	1964	24·4
1946	2·0		
1947	2·95	1965	26·4
1948	4·07	1966	27·7
1949	5·08	1967	29·6
		1968	31·8
		1969	32·6
		1970	34·6
		1971	36·2

* Excluding bicycle tyres.

Sources: *Nar. Khoz. 1959*, 206; *1964*, 180; *1968*, 253; *1970*, 203
Promyshlennost' SSSR (1957), 199

31. MACHINERY AND METALWORKING

(index of gross output)

	Machinery and metalworking		*Machinery and metalworking*	*of which, machinery*
1913	**100**	1940	**100**	**100**
1928	175	1945	129	131
1929	238	1946	85	80
1930	387	1950	215	235
1931	588	1951	252	282
1932	699 (732)*	1952	292	329
1933	804	1953	339	395
1934	1011	1954	393	469
1935	1307	1955	466	568
		1956	530	662
1937	1977	1957	600	770
1940	2963	1958	683	882
		1959	786	1020
		1960	904	1183
		1961	1039	1373
		1962	1197	1591
		1963	1353	1807
		1964	1482	1973
		1965	1622	2164
		1966	1814	2439
		1967	2037	2752
		1968	2279	3084
		1969	2546	3451
		1970	2831	3838

Sources: *Nar. Khoz. 1970*, 204
Promyshlennost' SSSR (1964), 245
Sots. Stroi (1936), xxii–xxiii (indices for 1929–34 calculated from figures in this volume)

* Different sources give slightly different figures.

32. MACHINE TOOLS

(metal-cutting lathes)

(000)

1913	1·5[x]	1950	70·6
	1·8[y]	1951	71·2
		1952	74·6
1917	0·2	1953	91·8
1928	2·0	1954	102·4
1929	4·3	1955	117·1
1930	8·0	1956	124·0
1931	18·2	1957	131·0
1932	19·7	1958	138·3
1933	21·0	1959	147·6
1934	25·4	1960	155·9
1935	33·9	1961	165·8
1936	44·4	1962	176·8
1937	48·5	1963	182·7
1938	55·3	1964	184·4
1939	55·0	1965	186·1
1940	58·4	1966	192·2
		1967	197·0
1945	38·4	1968	200·8
1946	40·3	1969	205·3
1947	50·4		
1948	64·5	1970	202·3
1949	64·9	1971	205

Sources: *Nar. Khoz. 1969*, 220; *1970*, 209
Pravda (23 January 1972)
Promyshlennost' SSSR (1964), 255
SSSR i Zarubezhnye strany: stat. sbor. (1970), 44

33. TURBINES

	all turbines (steam, gas and water) units	all turbines capacity (000 KW)	of which, water turbines units	water turbines capacity (000 KW)		all turbines (steam, gas and water) units	all turbines capacity (000 KW)	of which, water turbines units	water turbines capacity (000 KW)
1913	—	5·9	0	0	1950	1622	2704·0	1342	314·9
1928	47	44·1	30	8·4	1951	1065	3149·6	550	478·2
1929			55	11·6	1952	649	3452·4	157	571·5
1930			40	28·5	1953	986	4759·4	135	718·9
1931	56	250·5	22	42·8	1954	1005	5468·5	193	1261·7
1932	57	298·5	27	59·5	1955	556	5571·2	182	1491·9
1933	77	687·4	36	52·9	1956	461	5862·2		1580·6
1934			25	72·9	1957	457	5382·1		1308·4
1935			55	52·9	1958	474	6646·6		1225·7
1936			89	74·1	1959	504	7594·1		1412·1
1937	112	1156·1	59	88·3	1960	487	9199·9		1737·8
1938	132	1187·6	69	52·5	1961	373	10,732·2		2347·3
1939	133	1521·6	45	144·8	1962	324	11,899·5		2558·8
1940	146	1179·5	89	207·7	1963	349	11,871·6		1750·3
1945	422	229·9	414	40·6	1964	351	13,257		
1946	1795	441·9	1788	196·7	1965	342	14,625		
1947	1717	941·5	1696	323·9	1966	332	15,172		
1948	1414	1059·9	1386	336·3	1967	321	14,684		
1949	1393	1581·9	1332	339·9	1968	327	15,746		
					1969	306	15,004		
					1970	326	16,191		
					1971		16,800		

Sources: *Nar. Khoz. 1969*, 219; *1970*, 207
Pravda (23 January 1972)
Promyshlennost' SSSR (1957), 217; (1964), 252
Sots. Stroi. (1935), 38

34. FORGING AND PRESSING MACHINES*

(units)

1932	1125	1955	17,117
		1956	19,620
1937	3125	1957	22,950
1938	4183	1958	26,163
1939	4989	1959	29,276
1940	4668	1960	29,933
1945	2871	1961	30,520
1946	3386	1962	33,434
1947	4622	1963	34,221
1948	6880	1964	34,497
1949	5917	1965	34,637
1950	7684	1966	38,412
1951	9270	1967	41,126
1952	9603	1968	42,128
1953	11,200	1969	42,658
1954	13,544	1970	41,268
		1971	42,300

* Excluding hand machines.

Sources: *Nar. Khoz. 1970*, 209
Pravda (23 January 1972)
Promyshlennost' SSSR (1964), 256–7

35. MOTOR VEHICLES

(000 units)

	Total	*Lorries*	*Cars*	*Buses*
1924	0·010			
1925	0·116			
1926	0·366			
1927	0·478			
1928	0·841	0·791*	0·05	—
1929	1·7	1·6*		—
1930	4·2	4·1*		—
1931	4·0	4·0*	—	—
1932	23·9	23·7	0·034	0·1
1933	49·7	39·5*	10·3	—
1934	72·4	55·3*	17·1	—
1935	96·7	77·7*	19·0	—
1936	136·5	132·8*	3·7	—
1937	199·9	180·3	18·3	1·3
1938	211·1	184·1*	27·0	—
1939	201·7	182·0*	19·6	—
1940	145·5	136·0	5·5	3·9
1945	74·7	68·5	5·0	1·1
1946	102·2	94·6	6·3	1·3
1947	133·0	123·3*	9·6	—
1948	197·1	176·9*	20·2	—
1949	276·0	230·3*	45·7	—
1950	362·9	294·4	64·6	3·9
1951	288·7	235·0*	53·6	—
1952	307·9	248·3*	59·7	—
1953	354·2	276·8*	77·4	—
1954	403·9	309·1*	94·7	—
1955	445·3	328·0	107·8	9·4
1956	464·6	366·8*	97·8	—
1957	495·4	381·8*	113·6	—
1958	511·1	374·9	122·2	14·0
1959	495·0	351·4	124·5	19·1

* Including buses, not available separately.

35. MOTOR VEHICLES (continued)

(000 units)

	Total	*Lorries*	*Cars*	*Buses*
1960	523·6	362·0	138·8	22·8
1961	555·3	381·6	148·9	24·8
1962	577·5	382·4	165·9	29·2
1963	587·0	382·2	173·1	31·7
1964	603·1	385·0	185·2	32·9
1965	616·3	379·6	201·2	35·5
1966	675·2	407·6	230·3	37·3
1967	728·8	437·4	251·4	40·0
1968	800·8	478·1	280·3	42·4
1969	844·2	504·5	293·6	46·1
1970	916·1	524·5	344·2	47·4
1971	1142·7	564·3	529·0	49·4

Sources: *Nar. Khoz. 1959*, 216; *1965*, 200; *1968*, 261; *1970*, 217
Pravda (23 January 1972)
Promyshlennost' SSSR (1964), 278

36. TRACTORS

	000 units	*15* HP *units*		*000 units*	*15* HP *units*
1923	(2 tractors)		1950	116·7	246·1
1924	(11 tractors)		1951	93·1	207·2
			1952	98·9	219·3
1925	0·6	0·4	1953	111·3	245·8
1926	0·9	0·6	1954	135·4	274·3
1927	0·9	0·6			
1928	1·3	1·8	1955	163·4	314·0
1929	3·3	3·6	1956	183·5	352·1
			1957	203·8	384·0
1930	9·1	9·1	1958	219·7	415·3
1931	37·9	35·1	1959	213·5	418·2
1932	48·9	50·8			
1933	73·7	79·9	1960	238·5	475·4
1934	94·0	118·1	1961	263·6	548·9
			1962	287·0	606·9
1935	112·6	155·5	1963	325·3	683·5
1936	112·9	173·6	1964	329·0	720·5
1937	51·0	77·2			
1938	49·2	93·4	1965	354·5	803·8
1939	48·1	88·8	1966	382·5	879·3
			1967	405·1	951·5
1940	31·6	66·2	1968	423·4	1006
1945	7·7	14·7	1969	441·7	1111
1946	13·3	28·4			
1947	27·8	65·4	1970	458·5	1146
1948	56·9	144·2	1971	472	
1949	93·3	195·9			

Sources: *Nar. Khoz. 1970*, 218
Pravda (23 January 1972)
Promyshlennost' SSSR (1964), 279

37. GRAIN COMBINE HARVESTERS

(000 units)

1928	—	1955	48·0
		1956	81·8
1930	0·1	1957	131·5
1931	3·55	1958	65·0
1932	10·0	1959	54·7
1933	8·58		
1934	8·24	1960	59·0
		1961	76·3
1935	20·2	1962	79·8
1937	43·9	1963	82·9
		1964	83·6
1940	12·8		
		1965	85·8
1945	0·3	1966	92·0
		1967	101·2
1950	46·3	1968	101·3
1951	53·3	1969	94·5
1952	42·2		
1953	43·1	1970	99·2
1954	38·6	1971	102

Sources: *Nar. Khoz. 1958*, 244; *1959*, 218; *1964*, 188; *1968*, 263; *1969*, 226; *1970*, 219
Pravda (23 January 1972)
Promyshlennost' SSSR (1957), 230–1; (1964), 280–1
Sots. Stroi. (1936), 162

38. TIMBER

(m. cubic metres)

	Total	Commercial*		Total	Commercial*
1913	67·0[y]	30·5[y]	1950	266·0	161·0
	60·6[x]	27·2[x]	1951	296·7	184·5
			1952	291·4	184·6
1928	61·7	36·0	1953	292·1	179·9
1929	95·5	60·0	1954	328·9	205·8
1930	147·2	96·7	1955	333·9	212·1
1931	159·8	104·1	1956	342·3	222·1
1932	164·7	99·4	1957	361·4	237·8
1933	173·3	98·0	1958	375·0	250·9
1934	181·3	99·7	1959	397·8	270·1
1935	210·1	117·0	1960	369·5	261·5
1936	221·9	128·1	1961	351·0	253·3
1937	209·0	114·2	1962	352·7	255·7
1938	223·1	114·7	1963	369·6	267·3
1939	264·1	126·1	1964	385·3	276·9
1940	246·1	117·9	1965	378·1	273·6
1945	168·4	61·6	1966	373·5	271·7
1946	185·5	80·3	1967	383·0	286·9
1947	201·9	99·0	1968	380·4	289·9
1948	249·7	132·4	1969	374·2	286·3
1949	269·0	151·3	1970	385·1	298·6
			1971		288

* 'Total' timber produced includes firewood—'commercial' excludes this.

Sources: *Nar. Khoz. 1970*, 222
Pravda (23 January 1972)
Promyshlennost' SSSR (1964), 294

39. CELLULOSE, PAPER AND CARDBOARD

(000 tons)

	Cellulose	*Paper*	*Cardboard*
1913	257·6[y]	269·2[y]	40·8[y]
	40·7[x]	197·0[x]	29·4[x]
1917		155	
1921		32·2	1·94
1922		40·2	3·67
1923		62·1	11·8
1924		120·0	16·6
1925	55·0	211·0	23·5
1926	68·0	254·0	33·0
1927	75·6	268·0	44·5
1928	86·0	284·5	47·1
1929	126·1	384·9	62·5
1930	172·0	495·3	77·0
1931	185·0	505·2	62·0
1932	185·2	471·2	73·0
1933	206·3	506·1	79·0
1934	239·0	565·8	91·5
1935	271·2	640·8	107·8
1936	371·9	763·5	133·2
1937	425·6	831·6	144·2
1938	440·6	832·8	149·2
1939	463·5	799·8	159·0
1940	528·8	812·4	150·8
1945	275·9	321·1	55·7
1946	328·4	516·7	97·5
1947	507·9	647·5	140·8
1948	689·4	778·6	180·5
1949	946·7	995·4	232·1

39. CELLULOSE, PAPER AND CARDBOARD (continued)

(000 tons)

	Cellulose	*Paper*	*Cardboard*
1950	1099·8	1180·3	304·8
1951	1261·0	1341·7	333·9
1952	1407·8	1461·2	383·7
1953	1559·0	1611·6	442·5
1954	1680·5	1769·2	499·3
1955	1741·5	1847·8	559·8
1956	1845·1	1993·5	587·7
1957	1967·0	2125·7	656·6
1958	2092·7	2235·9	720·5
1959	2186·9	2326·5	764·2
1960	2281·6	2333·7	893·1
1961	2415·0	2494·1	951·4
1962	2595·3	2664·8	1003·3
1963	2757·7	2760·2	1092·9
1964	2933·1	2899·6	1220·4
1965	3234·3	3230·7	1449·0
1966	3598·8	3568·1	1662·1
1967	4031·1	3800·7	1875·8
1968	4341·0	3954·9	2014·5
1969	4615·4	4046·2	2238·0
1970	5109·5	4185·3	2516·0
1971	5400	4400	2700

Sources: *Nar. Khoz. 1932*, 8–9; *1970*, 227
Pravda (23 January 1972)
Promyshlennost' SSSR (1964), 302
SSSR i Zarubezhnye strany: stat. sbor., 45

40. CEMENT

(*m. tons*)

Year	Output	Year	Output
1913	1·777[y]	1945	1·845
	1·520[x]	1946	3·373
1917	0·963	1947	4·718
		1948	6·455
1920	0·036	1949	8·147
1921	0·064	1950	10·194
1922	0·142	1951	12·070
1923	0·271	1952	13·910
1924	0·392	1953	15·961
1925	0·872	1954	18·992
1926	1·403	1955	22·484
1927	1·574	1956	24·858
1928	1·850	1957	28·896
1929	2·232	1958	33·308
1930	3·006	1959	38·781
1931	3·336	1960	45·520
1932	3·478	1961	50·964
1933	2·709	1962	57·328
1934	3·536	1963	61·018
1935	4·488	1964	64·934
1936	5·872	1965	72·388
1937	5·454	1966	80·013
1938	5·688	1967	84·809
1939	5·197	1968	87·512
1940	5·675	1969	89·740
		1970	95·248
		1971	100·3

Sources: *Nar. Khoz. 1970*, 230
Promyshlennost' SSSR (1964), 318
Pravda (23 January 1972)

41. FABRICS

*(m. square metres)**

	Total†	*Cotton*	*Wool*	*Linen*	*Silk*	*Jute*
1913	2124[x]	1756[x]	132[x]	120[x]	35[xy]	81[xy]
	2192[y]	1817[y]	138[y]	121[y]		
1917	1212	952 (1400)	90 (70)	97 (97)	15 (18)	58
1918	[(1132)]	(991)	(61)	(80)		
1919	[(219)]	(153)	(24)	(42)	(0·6)	
1920	[(165)]	(120)	(18)	(27)	(0·4)	
1921	[(22)]	(157)	(14)	(30)	(0·7)	
1922	[(557)]	(434)	(29)	(91)	(2·5)	
1923	[(852)]	(719)	(36)	(93)	(4·2)	
1924	[(1194)]	(1032)	(41)	(118)	(2·6)	
1925	[(1896)]	(1698)	(58)	(137)	(2·5)	
1926	[(2577)]	(2313)	(75)	(183)	(6)	
1927	[(2683)]	(2397)	(95)	(184)	(7)	
1928	2198	1821 (2678)	112 (87)	177 (174)	8 (9)	80
1929	[2357]	2037	129	180	11	
1930	[1947]	1599	147	186	15	
1931	[1820]	1525	139	140	16	
1932	2164	1832	114	136	18	64
1933	[2134]	1858	111	143	22	
1934	[2155]	1869	100	160	26	
1935	[2166]	1816	108	210	32	
1936	[2709]	2253	130	283	43	
1937	3013	2431	139	274	49	120
1938	[2901]	2457	144	251	49	
1939	[3109]	2649	155	246	59	
1940	3299	2704	152	268	64	111

* Figures in round brackets for 1917–28 are in linear metres.

† Totals in square brackets exclude jute.

41. FABRICS (continued)

(m. square metres)

	Total†	*Cotton*	*Wool*	*Linen*	*Silk*	*Jute*
1945	1353	1149	65	98	29	12
1946	1590	1338	87	105	39	21
1947	[2075]	1774	118	130	53	
1948	[2588]	2211	151	159	67	
1949	[3009]	2531	184	208	86	
1950	3374	2745	193	257	106	73
1951	[3982]	3337	222	281	142	
1952	[4198]	3551	240	227	180	
1953	[4582]	3752	262	256	312	
1954	[4949]	3985	305	255	404	
1955	5347	4227	316	272	415	117
1956	[5266]	3972	339	353	602	
1957	[5496]	4095	359	388	654	
1958	[5823]	4308	385	440	690	
1959	[6178]	4615	415	485	663	
1960	6636	4838	439	516	675	168
1961	6650	4875	454	493	682	146
1962	6811	4914	469	485	787	156
1963	7011	5071	471	509	801	159
1964	7377	5366	472	544	832	163
1965	7472	5499	466	548	801	158
1966	7827	5703	510	592	869	153
1967	8193	5916	547	642	938	150
1968	8470	6116	585	676	950	143
1969	8659	6208	618	674	1026	133
1970	8774	6152	643	707	1146	126
1971	[9022]	6397	675	760	1190	

† Totals in square brackets exclude jute.

Sources: *Nar. Khoz. 1970*, 239
Pravda (23 January 1972)
Promyshlennost' SSSR (1964), 364
SSSR i Zarubezhnye strany: stat. sbor., 50–1

42. KNITWEAR

(*m. units*)

	Total	Outer	Under		Total	Outer	Under
1928	8·3	1·4	6·9	1955	432	85·2	346·5
1932	39	11·7	27·3	1956	434	85·4	348·5
1933	53	17·2	36·1	1957	465	90·2	374·7
1934	76	22·4	53·7	1958	497	97·2	399·3
1935	89	26·0	63·2	1959	543	103·9	438·6
1936	122	35·9	85·9	1960	584	111·6	472·3
1937	157	45·1	111·5	1961	606	117·8	487·7
1938	169	54·0	114·9	1962	644	124·9	519·4
1939	171	53·7	117·0	1963	687	132·9	554·5
1940	183	58·6	124·4	1964	793	153·4	639·8
1945	50	23·4	26·6	1965	906	187·9	718·3
1946	76	30·4	46·0	1966	992	222·1	770·4
1947	100	38·9	61·3	1967	1067	255·4	811·8
1948	127	42·9	84·3	1968	1128	302·7	825·0
1949	164	45·1	118·6	1969	1185	363·4	821·6
1950	198	47·1	150·4	1970	1236	415·2	821·2
1951	257	58·9	198·3	1971	1275	444	831
1952	298	63·5	234·9				
1953	341	66·0	274·7				
1954	403	75·5	327·1				

Sources: *Nar. Khoz. 1964*, 220–1; *1969*, 254; *1970*, 243–4
Pravda (23 January 1972)
Promyshlennost' SSSR (1964), 384

43. FOOTWEAR (LEATHER)

(m. pairs)

Year			Year	
1913	68^{y}		1945	63·1
	60^{x}		1946	81·2
1917	50		1947	112·8
			1948	134·0
1921		(3·4)*	1949	163·6
1922		(3·4)	1950	203·0
1923		(4·5)	1951	239·2
1924		(5·1)	1952	237·0
1925		(9·1)	1953	238·1
1926		(12·0)	1954	255·2
1927		(18·9)	1955	271·2
1928	58·0	(24·4)	1956	287·0
1929	77·0	(39·3)	1957	317·3
1930	75·4	(61·1)	1958	356·4
1931	86·7		1959	389·9
1932	86·9		1960	419·3
1933	90·3		1961	443·2
1934	85·4		1962	456·3
1935	103·6		1963	462·7
1936	143·2		1964	474·7
1937	182·9		1965	486·0
1938	192·9		1966	522·2
1939	205·7		1967	561·3
1940	211·0		1968	597·6
			1969	635·8
			1970	675·7
			1971	679

* Figures in brackets relate to large-scale industry only.

Sources: *Nar. Khoz. 1932*, 8–9; *1969*, 256; *1970*, 245
Pravda (23 January 1972)
Promyshlennost' SSSR (1964), 394
SSSR i Zarubezhnye Strany: stat. sbor., 45

44. FURNITURE

(*m. rubles*)

1940	—
1950	—
1952	288
1953	331
1954	425
1955	491
1956	528
1957	613
1958	755
1959	942
1960	1116
1961	1292
1962	1453
1963	1598
1964	1696
1965	1828
1966	1997
1967	2201/2171*
1968	2423/2390*
1969	2559
1970	2794
1971	3100

* First figure in 1955 prices; second figure in 1967 prices. (Up to 1966 figures are in 1955 prices; from 1969 in 1967 prices.)

Sources: *Nar. Khoz. 1964*, 225; *1968*, 300; *1970*, 252
Pravda (23 January 1972)
Promyshlennost' SSSR (1964), 411

45. WASHING MACHINES

	(*units*)
1940	—
1948	—
1949	10
1950	300
	(*000 units*)
1951	1·9
1952	4·3
1953	3·5
1954	45·7
1955	87·0
1956	181·9
1957	338·0
1958	463·7
1959	647·8
1960	895·5
	(*m. units*)
1961	1·29
1962	1·80
1963	2·28
1964	2·86
1965	3·43
1966	3·87
1967	4·32
1968	4·70
1969	5·15
1970	5·24
1971	4·1

Sources: *Nar. Khoz. 1964*, 224; *1968*, 198–9; *1969*, 263; *1970*, 251
Pravda (23 January 1972)
Promyshlennost' SSSR (1964), 408

46. REFRIGERATORS

	(units)
1940	3500
1945	300
1946	—
1947	—
1948	300
1949	1800
1950	1200
1951	15,000
1952	31,100
1953	49,200
1954	94,000
	(000 units)
1955	151·4
1956	224·0
1957	308·9
1958	359·6
1959	426·1
1960	529·5
1961	686·5
1962	837·8
1963	910·6
	(m. units)
1964	1·13
1965	1·68
1966	2·21
1967	2·70
1968	3·16
1969	3·70
1970	4·14
1971	4·6

Sources: *Nar. Khoz. 1964*, 224; *1968*, 198–9, 299; *1969*, 263; *1970*, 251
Pravda (23 January 1972)
Promyshlennost' SSSR (1964), 408

47. VACUUM CLEANERS

(*000 units*)

1940	—
1945	1·1
1946	0·6
1947	0·2
1948	0·5
1949	2·0
1950	6·1
1951	15·3
1952	22·5
1953	45·5
1954	131·6
1955	130·9
1956	174·7
1957	261·7
1958	245·2
1959	367·5
1960	500·8
1961	535·9
1962	625·5
1963	726·7
1964	764·5
1965	800
1966	899
1967	1097
1968	1230
1969	1359
1970	1509

Sources: *Nar. Khoz. 1964*, 224; *1968*, 198–9, 299; *1969*, 263; *1970*, 251
Promyshlennost' SSSR (1964), 408

48. TELEVISION SETS

	(*units*)
1939	10
1940	300
1945	—
1946	—
1947	200
1948	4200
1949	1800
	(*000 units*)
1950	11·9
1951	25·3
1952	37·4
1953	84·1
1954	254·3
1955	494·7
1956	596·2
1957	707·8
1958	979·4
	(*m. units*)
1959	1·28
1960	1·73
1961	1·95
1962	2·17
1963	2·47
1964	2·93
1965	3·66
1966	4·42
1967	4·96
1968	5·74
1969	6·60
1970	6·68
1971	5·8

Sources: *Nar. Khoz. 1964*, 224; *1968*, 198–9, 299; *1969*, 263; *1970*, 251
Pravda (23 January 1972)
Promyshlennost' SSSR (1964), 407

49. RADIOS AND RADIOGRAMS

	(000 units)		(m. units)
1928	—	1950	1·07
		1951	1·23
1932	29·3	1952	1·30
1933	25·7	1953	1·64
1934	50·8	1954	2·90
1935	130·1	1955	3·55
1936	322·7	1956	3·77
1937	199·9	1957	3·55
1938	203·2	1958	3·90
1939	180·8	1959	4·03
1940	160·5	1960	4·17
1945	13·9	1961	4·23
1946	228·6	1962	4·25
1947	380·4	1963	4·80
1948	536·6	1964	4·77
1949	888·0	1965	5·16
		1966	5·84
		1967	6·42
		1968	6·98
		1969	7·27
		1970	7·82
		1971	8·8

Sources: *Nar. Khoz. 1964*, 224; *1968*, 198–9, 299; *1969*, 263; *1970*, 251
Pravda (23 January 1972)
Promyshlennost' SSSR (1964), 407

50. CAMERAS

(000 units)

1930	3·0	1950	260·6
1931	23·0	1951	357·5
1932	29·6	1952	459·4
1933	115·4	1953	499·5
1934	168·6	1954	768·7
1935	151·9	1955	1023
1936	256·8	1956	1196
1937	353·2	1957	1323
1938	335·9	1958	1473
1939	478·6	1959	1616
1940	355·2	1960	1764
		1961	1398
1945	0·01	1962	1339
1946	5·7	1963	1431
1947	91·5	1964	1166
1948	156·4		
1949	166·2	1965	1053
		1966	1420
		1967	1588
		1968	1841
		1969	1961
		1970	2045

Sources: *Nar. Khoz. 1964*, 224; *1967*, 305; *1969*, 263; *1970*, 251
Promyshlennost' SSSR (1964), 409

51. SEWING MACHINES

(000 units)

1913	271·8	1955	1611
1928	285·6	1956	1914
1932	318·8	1957	2267
1937	510·1	1958	2686
1940	175·2	1959	2941
1945	—	1960	3096
1946	16·0	1961	3292
1947	125·0	1962	3341
1948	309·2	1963	2602
1949	413·9	1964	1564
1950	501·7	1965	800
1951	668·0	1966	1025
1952	804·5	1967	1198
1953	993·2	1968	1300
1954	1281	1969	1324
		1970	1400

Sources: *Nar. Khoz. 1964*, 224; *1967*, 305; *1968*, 198–9, 299; *1969*, 263; *1970*, 251
Promyshlennost' SSSR (1964), 408

52. CLOCKS AND WATCHES

(*m. units*)

	Total	of which, wrist watches		Total	of which, wrist watches
1913	0·7	—	1950	7·57	1·53
			1951	9·65	2·28
1917	0·7	—			
			1952	10·5	2·92
1928	0·9	—	1953	12·8	4·20
1929		—	1954	16·4	5·59
1930	0·233	—	1955	19·7	8·03
1931	2·99	—	1956	22·6	10·5
1932	3·56	—	1957	23·5	13·2
1933	4·09	—	1958	24·8	15·1
1934	4·37	—	1959	26·2	16·2
1935	4·50	—	1960	26·0	16·3
1936	4·94	—	1961	26·0	15·2
1937	4·03	—	1962	26·1	14·7
1938	3·54	0·005	1963	27·1	14·5
1939	2·98	0·149	1964	28·7	14·6
1940	2·80	0·210	1965	30·6	14·8
			1966	32·4	16·1
1945	0·336	0·066			
			1967	34·4	17·8
1946	0·567	0·088			
			1968	36·3	19·1
1947	1·24	0·156			
			1969	38·0	20·5
1948	3·04	0·518			
1949	5·93	1·09	1970	40·2	21·7
			1971	42·1	

Sources: *Nar. Khoz. 1964*, 224; *1968*, 196–7, 299; *1969*, 263; *1970*, 251
Pravda (23 January 1972)
Promyshlennost' SSSR (1964), 406

53. MOTORCYCLES

(including scooters)

(*000 units*)

1913	0·1	1955	245
		1956	297
1928	—	1957	337
1932	0·1	1958	400
		1959	500
1937	13·1		
		1960	553
1940	6·8	1961	588
1945	4·7	1962	621
1946	6·1	1963	647
1947	30	1964	687
1948	68		
		1965	721
1949	92	1966	753
1950	123	1967	284
1951	125	1968	802
1952	104	1969	808
1953	143		
		1970	833
1954	206	1971	872

Sources: *Nar. Khoz. 1964*, 224; *1968*, 198–9; *1970*, 251
Pravda (23 January 1972)
Promyshlennost' SSSR (1964), 410

54. FISH

(000 tons)

1913	1018[x]	1945	1125
	1051[y]	1946	1208
1917	893	1947	1534
		1948	1575
1919	170	1949	1953
1920	257	1950	1755
1921	298	1951	2142
1922	483	1952	2107
1923	499	1953	2195
1924	535	1954	2505
1925	721	1955	2737
1926	897	1956	2849
1927	747	1957	2761
1928	840	1958	2936
1929	956	1959	3075
1930	1283	1960	3541
1931	1441	1961	3724
1932	1333	1962	4168
1933	1303	1963	4681
1934	1547	1964	5171
1935	1520	1965	5774
1936	1631	1966	6093
1937	1609	1967	6538
1938	1542	1968	6784
1939	1566	1969	7091
1940	1404	1970	7900

Sources: *Nar. Khoz. 1970*, 257
Promyshlennost' SSSR (1964), 437
SSSR i Zarubezhnye Strany: stat. sbor., 51

55. PRESERVES

(m. standard tins)

1913	95[x]	1950	1535
	116[y]	1951	1848
		1952	2064
1928	125	1953	2358
1929	240	1954	2741
1930	320	1955	3217
1931	420	1956	3601
1932	692	1957	3794
1933	619	1958	4073
1934	722	1959	4363
1935	808	1960	4864
1936	1002	1961	5551
1937	982	1962	5914
1938	1104	1963	6470
1939	1148	1964	7452
1940	1113	1965	7078
1945	558	1966	7541
1946	583	1967	8908
1947	669	1968	9548
1948	868	1969	9660
1949	1162	1970	10,676
		1971	11,300

Sources: *Nar. Khoz. 1970*, 260
Promyshlennost' SSSR (1964), 447

III. AGRICULTURE

56. SOWN AREA†

1. Crop structure

(m. hectares)

	Total	*Grain**	*Wheat*	*Rye*	*Barley*	*Oats*	*Grain* Maize*
1913	105·0[x]	94·4[x]	31·6[x]	25·8[x]	11·5[x]	16·9[x]	1·4[x]
	118·2[y]	104·6[y]	33·0[y]	28·2[y]	12·7[y]	19·1[y]	2·2[y]
1920	97·2	87·0	27·7	23·5	9·4	14·9	1·7
1921	90·3	79·8	23·5	24·0	9·0	12·8	1·8
1922	77·7	66·2	14·4	23·0	4·6	9·5	3·2
1923	91·7	78·6	18·4	27·1	7·6	11·6	2·5
1924	98·1	82·9	22·0	28·1	7·4	12·9	2·5
1925	104·3	87·3	24·9	28·8	6·5	12·8	3·4
1926	110·3	93·7	29·4	28·5	7·4	15·3	3·0
1927	112·4	94·7	31·2	27·3	6·9	17·9	2·7
1928	113·0	92·2	27·7	24·6	7·3	17·2	4·5
1929	118·0	96·0	29·7	24·9	8·1	18·9	3·5
1930	127·2	101·8	33·7	28·0	7·4	17·9	3·7
1931	136·3	104·4	36·9	27·7	6·8	17·5	4·0
1932	134·4	99·7	34·5	25·8	6·8	15·4	3·7
1933	129·7	101·5	33·2	25·4	7·3	16·7	4·0
1934	131·5	104·7	35·2	24·0	8·5	18·0	3·7
1935	132·8	103·4	37·1	23·5	8·7	18·3	3·2
1936	133·8	102·6					
1937	135·3	104·5	41·4	22·7	9·2	17·6	2·8
1938	136·9	102·4	41·5				
1939	133·7	99·9					
1940	150·6	110·7	40·3	23·1	10·5	20·2	3·7

[x] Pre-1939 territory [y] Present territory (otherwise area for territory of given years)

* See footnote on page 101. This column includes the crops in the next five columns.

† Sown area is the area actually sown when the spring sowing has been completed.

56. SOWN AREA (Continued)

1. Crop structure (continued)

(*m. hectares*)

	*Technical Crops**	*Cotton*	*Sugar beet*	*Potatoes and vegetables*	*Feed Crops*	*Feed Maize*
1913	4·5[x]	0·69[x]	0·65[x]	3·8[x]	2·1[x]	—
	4·9[y]	0·69[y]	0·68[y]	5·1[y]	3·3[y]	—
1920		0·099	0·20	3·7†	—	—
1921		0·099	0·22	3·8†		
1922		0·070	0·18	3·9†		
1923		0·22	0·26	4·3†		
1924		0·45	0·38	4·7†		
1925		0·59	0·53	5·0†		
1926		0·65	0·54	5·2†		
1927		0·80	0·67	5·5†		
1928	8·6	0·97	0·77	7·7	3·9	
1929	8·8	1·06	0·77	7·6	5·0	
1930	10·5	1·58	1·04	8·0	6·5	
1931	14·0	2·14	1·39	9·1	8·8	
1932	14·9	2·17	1·54	9·2	10·6	
1933	12·0	2·05	1·21	8·7	7·3	
1934	10·7	1·94	1·18	8·8	7·1	
1935	10·6	1·95	1·23	9·9	8·6	
1936	10·8			9·8	10·6	
1937	11·2	2·12	1·19	9·0	10·6	
1938	11·0	2·08	1·18	9·4	14·1	
1939	11·1			9·2	13·5	
1940	11·8	2·08	1·23	10·0	18·1	

† Potatoes only. * These include cotton and sugar beet.

56. SOWN AREA (continued)

1. Crop structure (continued)

(m. hectares)

	Total	*Grain**	*Wheat*	*Rye*	*Barley*	*Oats*	*Grain* Maize*
1945	113·8	85·3	24·9	20·3	10·4	14·4	4·2
1946	114·0	85·9					
1947	119·9	90·9					
1948	133·7	100·9					
1949	139·7	102·6					
1950	146·3	102·9	38·5	23·6	8·6	16·2	4·8
1951	153·0	106·4					
1952	155·7	107·3					
1953	157·2	106·7	48·3	20·3	9·6	15·3	3·5
1954	166·1	112·1	49·3	20·5	10·6	15·9	4·3
1955	185·8	123·5	60·5	19·1	9·8	14·8	6·2
1956	194·7	125·6	62·0	18·4	11·8	15·1	6·6
1957	193·7	122·1	69·0	18·1	9·2	14·0	3·3
1958	195·6	121·5	66·6	17·9	9·7	14·8	4·4
1959	196·3	114·5	63·0	17·1	9·7	14·3	3·5
1960	203·0	115·6	60·4	16·2	12·1	12·8	5·1
1961	204·6	122·3	63·0	16·7	13·4	11·5	7·2
1962	216·0	128·7	67·4	16·9	16·3	6·9	7·0
1963	218·5	130·0	64·6	15·0	20·4	5·7	7·0
1964	212·8	133·3	67·9	16·8	21·7	5·7	5·1
1965	209·1	128·0	70·2	16·0	19·7	6·6	3·2
1966	206·8	124·8	70·0	13·6	19·4	7·2	3·2
1967	206·9	122·2	67·0	12·4	19·1	8·7	3·5
1968	207·0	121·5	67·2	12·2	19·4	9·0	3·4
1969	208·6	122·7	66·4	9·2	22·5	9·3	4·2
1970	206·7	119·3	65·2	10·0	21·3	9·2	3·4

* Maize fully ripe only is included in grain—all others in fodder. Definitions of these vary from earlier to later volumes (earlier ones put milk wax stage into grain, not feed crops).

56. SOWN AREA (continued)

1. Crop structure (continued)

(*m. hectares*)

	Technical crops	*Cotton*	*Sugar beet*	*Potatoes and vegetables*	*Feed crops*	*Feed* Maize*
1945	7·7	1.21	0·83	10·6	10.2	—
1946						
1947						
1948						
1949						
1950	12·2	2·32	1·31	10·5	20·7	—
1951						
1952						
1953	11·5	1·88	1·57	10·3	28·7	
1954	11·8	2·20	1·60	11·0	31·2	
1955	12·3	2·20	1·76	11·4	38·6	11·7
1956	13·1	2·07	2·01	11·6	44·4	17·3
1957	11·8	2·09	2·11	11·9	47·9	15·0
1958	12·3	2·15	2·50	11·6	50·2	15·3
1959	12·4	2·15	2·75	11·6	57·8	18·9
1960	13·1	2·19	3·04	11·2	63·1	23·1
1961	13·6	2·33	3·12	10·8	57·9	18·5
1962	14·3	2·39	3·17	10·7	62·3	30·1
1963	14·9	2·48	3·75	10·5	63·1	27·2
1964	15·5	2·46	4·11	10·6	53·4	22·3
1965	15·3	2·44	3·88	10·6	55·2	20·2
1966	15·1	2·46	3·80	10·3	56·6	19·6
1967	14·8	2·44	3·80	10·3	59·6	19·6
1968	14·6	2·45	3·56	10·2	60·7	19·0
1969	14·4	2·54	3·39	10·0	61·5	18·5
1970	14·5	2·75	3·37	10·1	62·8	18·0

* included in feed crops

Sources: *Nar. Khoz. 1932*, 121, 162–3; *1958*, 386–9; *1961*, 311–12; *1964*, 267–8; *1967*, 348; *1969*, 308; *1970*, 294
Sel. Khoz. (1935), 238, 241, 262, 302, 317; (1960), 127; (1971), 108
Sots. Stroi. Soyuza SSR (1933–8), 95
Sots. Stroi. (1936), 280

56. SOWN AREA (continued)

2. Categories of farm

(*m. hectares*)

	Total	*State farms**	*Collective farms*	*Private plots†*
1913	105·0[x] 118·2[y]	—	—	—
1928	113·0	1·73	1·37	109·89
1929	118·0	2·27	4·15	111·62
1930	127·2	3·93	38·08	85·21
1931	136·3	10·96	78·97	46·35
1932	134·4	13·45	91·53	29·45
1933	129·7	14·14	93·64	21·91
1934	131·5	15·03	98·55	17·81
1935	132·8	16·19	104·51	11·96
1936	133·8			
1937	135·3			
1938	136·9	12·4	117·2	7·3
1939	133·7			
1940	150·63	13·26	117·72	19·65

* *Sovkhozy* and other state farms.

† Of collective farm members, workers, employees and other groups of the population.

56. SOWN AREA (continued)

2. Categories of farm (continued)

(*m. hectares*)

	Total	*State farms*	*Collective farms*	*Private plots*
1945	113·81	11·65	117·72	19·65
1946	114·0			
1947	119·9			
1948	133·7			
1949	139·7			
1950	146·30	15·92	121·01	9·37
1951	153·0			
1952	155·7			
1953	157·17	18·24	132·00	6·93
1954	166·1			
1955	185·85	29·37	149·06	7·42
1956	194·75	35·29	152·15	7·31
1957	193·7	53·97	132·41	7·29
1958	195·6	56·89	131·41	7·35
1959	196·3	58·81	130·27	7·24
1960	202·99	73·22	123·02	6·75
1961	204·62	87·28	110·60	6·73
1962	215·98	94·83	114·42	6·73
1963	218·52	97·81	113·99	6·72
1964	212·80	95·69	110·84	6·27
1965	209·10	97·43	105·07	6·60
1966	206·77	96·83	103·21	6·73
1967	206·84	97·09	102·98	6·77
1968	207·02	97·93	102·32	6·77
1969	208·60	101·51	100·31	6·78
1970	206·65	100·87	99·05	6·73

Sources: *Nar. Khoz. 1956*, 114; *1961*, 316; *1964*, 272; *1967*, 352; *1969*, 312; *1970*, 298
Sel. Khoz. (1935), 238
Sots. stroi. (1936), 295
Sots. stroi. Soyuza SSR (1933–8), 96

57. STATE FARMS*

	Number	*Average total land area (000 hectares)*	*Average livestock numbers* Cattle	Cows	Pigs	Sheep and goats	*Average labour force*
1928	1407						
1929	1536		133		35	783	271
1930	2832						
1931	3383						
1932	4337						
1933	4208		760		428	1355	576
1934	4118						
1935	4118	19·7	648	284	344	1305	371†
1938	3961		939		709	1774	383
1940	4159	12·2	592	229	459	1420	330
1950	4988	12·9	562	170	500	1530	
1953	4857	13·1	701	232	721	2084	380
1954	4874						

* Excluding co-operative farms (*koopkhozy*) (distinct from collective farms—*kolkhozy*) and agricultural enterprises of ORSy (workers' supply organisations).

† Workers only.

57. STATE FARMS (continued)

	Number	Average Total Land Area (000 hectares)	Average Livestock Numbers: Cattle	Cows	Pigs	Sheep and goats	Average Labour Force
1955	5134	14·9	652	249	647	2014	409
1956	5098	15·9	741	287	1038	2118	425
1957	5905	24·3	1207	424	1260	3975	543
1958	6002	24·9	1370	472	1355	4401	639
1959	6496	23·5	1633	547	1518	4532	645
1960	7375	26·2	1957	689	1715	4280	745
1961	8281	28·3	2310	799	1886	4664	794
1962	8570	28·3	2447	863	1956	4798	825
1963	9176	28·2	2356	865	827	4873	775
1964	10,078	27·2	2201	803	1144	4378	721
1965	11,681	24·6	2098	782	1073	3975	705
1966	12,189	23·7	2071	742	1049	4060	690
1967	12,783	22·8	2017	719	916	4040	658
1968	13,398	21·9	1927	687	865	3962	635
1969	14,310	21·4	1880	661	939	3499	613
1970	14,994	20·8	1939	696	1107	3567	593

Sources: *Nar. Khoz. 1956*, 147; *1961*, 455; *1962*, 352, 359; *1963*, 356, 359; *1964*, 410–11; *1968*, 438–9; *1969*, 285, 413; *1970*, 397–8
Sel. Khoz. (1935), 191; (1960), 36, 41, 49
Sots. Stroi. (1936), 260–1 (1935 figures calculated from this)
Sots. Stroi. Soyuza SSR (1933–8), 87 (figures for 1929, 1937, 1938 calculated from this)

58. COLLECTIVE FARMS

	Number* (000)	Average land area (000 hectares)	Average livestock† Cattle	Cows	Pigs	Sheep	Average house-holds
1928	33·3	0·096	5	2	2	7‡	13
1929	57·0		7	3	2	12‡	18
1930	85·9		42	16	10	65‡	70
1931	211·1	0·9	39	14	12	58‡	62
1932	211·1		47	14	15	57‡	71
1933	224·5		41	13	13	54‡	90
1934	233·3		42	13	16	61‡	95
1935	245·6						
1938	242·4						78
1940§	235·5	1·4	85	24	35	165	81
1950§	121·4		224	56	98	486	165
1952	94·8	4·0	313	88	166	743	208
1953	91·2	4·2	335	98	230	888	220
1954	87·1		355	115	253	905	224
1955	85·6	4·4	351	123	265	942	231
1956	83·0	4·5	369	135	306	989	238
1957	76·5	4·1	374	137	255	913‡	245
1958	67·7	4·5	463	166	334	1065	275
1959	53·4	5·5	674	233	490	1398	343

* Excluding fishing collectives; number at 1 June from 1928–35.
† In collective, not individual members', ownership.
§ I have been unable to find figures for 1945–9, but the policy of amalgamation started in 1949—so up till then numbers were basically as in 1940.
‡ Including goats.

58. COLLECTIVE FARMS (continued)

	*Number** *(000)*	*Average land area (000 hectares)*	*Average livestock†* *Cattle*	*Cows*	*Pigs*	*Sheep*	*Average house-holds*
1960	44·0	6·4	807	286	609	1587	383
1961	40·5	6·2	891	310	729	1624	399
1962	39·7	6·2	954	336	787	1645	404
1963	38·8	6·1	944	349	405	1534	411
1964	37·6	6·0	967	358	581	1390	418
1965	36·3	6·1	1038	371	667	1460	421
1966	36·5	6·0	1072	378	667	1491	417
1967	36·2	6·0	1092	386	599	1516	418
1968	35·6	6·0	1102	391	597	1541	420
1969	34·2	6·0	1156	404	714	1495	427
1970	33·0	6·1	1243	423	880	1611	431

Sources: *Nar. Khoz. 1956*, 140–1; *1959*, 423–4; *1960*, 492–3; *1962*, 330–1; *1963*, 341–2; *1964*, 390–1; *1967*, 466–7; *1969*, 285, 398; *1970*, 382–4
Sel. Khoz. (1935), 629 (average figures for livestock 1928–34 calculated from total data here); (1960), 41
Sots. Stroi. (1934), 164; (1936), 273
Sots. Stroi. Soyuza SSR (1933–8), 85

59. DELIVERIES OF INDUSTRIAL SUPPLIES

	Mineral fertiliser (m. tons, standard units)	*Tractors (000) (in 15 HP units)*	*Tractors (000) (=number of tractors)*	*Lorries (000)*	*Combines (000, grain, maize, and silage, but excluding sugar beet)*
1924/5		4·6	6·7		
1925/6		9·2	13·1		
1926/7		3·9	5·7		
1927/8		2·3	3·3		
1928/9		8·4	9·5		
1929/30		42·3	39·2		
1931		64·3	59·1		
1932	1·1	45·3	46·1		
1933	0·88	70·6	68·7	27·1	
1934	1·4	103·0	87·3	15·0	
1935	2·4	138·7*	103·1	13·4	
1940	3·2	33·5	20·3	17·5	12·8
1950	5·4	182·5	92·2	87·1	45·8
1953	6·6	151·1	76·2	68·9	41·5
1956	9·4				
1957	10·4				
1958	10·6	251·8	157·5	102·1	107·3
1959	11·1	236·3	144·3	76·3	66·2
1960	11·4	269·2	157·0	66·1	73·6
1961	12·1	333·9	185·3	69·7	108·0
1962	13·6	376·6	206·0	82·6	151·6
1963	16·0	437·7	239·3	68·8	163·8
1964	22·0	425·4	222·5	63·0	133·8
1965	27·1	482·1	239·5	70·2	102·3†
1966	30·5	583·1	276·0	105·5	98·5†
1967	33·7	623·7	287·4	108·1	113·9†
1968	37·5	644·2	290·3	113·8	117·6†
1969	38·8	696·3	304·3	125·9	115·5†
1970	45·6	721·1	309·3	125·8	130·0†
1971	50		312	143	145†

* Provisional figure.

† Excludes maize combines.

Sources: *Nar. Khoz. 1959*, 380; *1961*, 380, 417; *1964*, 338, 389; *1967*, 412, 465; *1968*, 422; *1969*, 357; *1970*, 339, 381
Pravda (23 January 1972)
Sel. Khoz. (1935), 199 (15 HP units calculated)
Sots. Stroi. (1936), 253, 353

60. GRAIN

Pre-war grain harvest figures from 1933 onwards were given in what was called 'biological yield', an estimate of the crop before it was harvested. The estimates were much higher than actual crop yields. The true figures for most years appeared in a specialised, very small circulation book (500 copies): Yu. Moshkov, *Zernovaya problema v gody sploshnoi kollektivizatsii* (Moscow University, 1966). Averages for 1933–7 and 1938–40 appear in post-1960 handbooks.

I have not been able to find procurement figures for 1925–7; this was the period before the beginning of the collectivisation drive, when, partly at least because the government cut grain prices substantially, peasants became increasingly reluctant to sell and procurements fell.

60. GRAIN (continued)

1. Harvest
(*m. tons*)

	All grains	*Wheat*	*Rye*	*Maize*
1913	80·1*			1·1 (2·1 in present territory)
1917	54·6			
1918	49·5			
1919	50·5			
1920	45·2			
1921	42·3 (36·2)†	9·5	—	—
1922	56·3§	11·8	18·2	3·0
1923	57·4	13·4	19·8	3·2
1924	51·4	13·1	18·8	2·3
1925	74·7	21·4	22·8	4·5
1926	78·3	24·9	23·7	3·5
1927	72·8	21·7	24·2	3·1
1928	73·3	22·0	19·3	3·3
1929	71·7	18·9	20·3	3·0
1930	83·5	26·9	23·6	2·7
1931	69·5	20·5	21·9	4·8
1932	69·6	20·3	22·0	3·4
1933	68·4 [89·8]**			
1934	67·6 [89·4]**			
1935	75·0 [90·1]**			
1936	56·1‡			
1937	97·4	38·9		2·8
1938	—§§	—		
1939	—§§	—		

* In pre-war territory according to pre-war source: post-war source gives 76·5 for this, and 86·0 for present-day territory.

† More than one figure exists for this year.

§ A figure of 50·3 is given in *Sotsialisticheskoe stroitelstvo* (1934), 4. Neither appears to be a misprint, as the full figures are 50·31 and 56·29.

** Figures in square brackets are 'biological yield'—see note preceding table.

‡ Calculated from other years and from average for 1933–7 in *Sel. Khoz. SSSR* (1960), 196.

§§ Annual average for 1938–40 was 77·9 (*Sel. Khoz.* (1960), 196). Since 1940 was 95·6, 1938–9 average must have been 69·0

60. GRAIN (continued)

1. Harvest (continued)

(m. tons)

	All grain	*Socialised sector (%)*	*Wheat*	*Rye*	*Maize (grain) (fully ripe)*
1940	95·6	(88)	31·8	21·1	5·2
1941	56·3				
1942	30·0				
1943	30·0				
1944	48·7				
1945	47·3	(81)	13·4		
1946	39·6				
1947	65·9				
1948	67·2				
1949	70·2				
1950	81·2	(93)	31·1	18·0	6·6
1951	78·7				
1952	92·2				
1953	82·5	(97)	41·3	14·5	3·7
1954	85·6		42·4		3·7
1955	103·7		47·3		11·6
1956	125·0		67·4		9·9
1957	102·6		58·1		4·6
1958	134·7	(98)	76·6	15·8	10·2
1959	119·5	(98)	69·1	16·9	5·7
1960	125·5	(98)	64·3	16·4	9·8
1961	130·8	(98)	66·5	16·7	17·1
1962	140·2	(98)	70·8	17·0	15·5
1963	107·5	(98)	49·7	11·9	11·1
1964	152·1	(99)	74·4	13·6	13·8
1965	121·1	(98)	59·7	16·2	8·0
1966	171·2	(98)	100·5	13·1	8·4
1967	147·9	(98)	77·4	13·0	9·2
1968	169·5	(98)	93·4	14·1	8·8
1969	162·4	(98)	79·9	10·9	12·0
1970	186·8	(99)	99·7	13·0	9·4
1971	181				

Sources: *Istoriya . . . 1941–45*, 67–9 (1941–4)
Moshkov, *Zernovaya Problema v gody sploshnoi kollektivizatsii* (Moscow, 1966), 226
Nar. Khoz. 1932, 121; *1958*, 418; *1961*, 300–1; *1963*, 273; *1964*, 302, 304; *1968*, 353, 354; *1969*, 323, 325, 327; *1970*, 281, 309, 311, 313, 314
Sel'. Khoz. 1935, 213; *1960*, 197
Sots. Stroi. (1934), 203

60. **GRAIN** (continued)

2. Procurements

(m. tons)

	All grains	*Wheat*
1917	1·7	
1918	1·8	
1919	3·5	
1920	6·0	
1921	3·8	
1922	6·9	
1923	6·5	
1924	5·2	
1925		
1926		
1927		
1928	10·8	5·3
1929	16·1	5·1
1930	22·1	9·0
1931	22·8	8·2
1932	18·5	5·8
1933	22·6	9·0
1934	26·1	9·3
1935	1933–7	1933–7
1936	average,	average,
	27·5	12·3
1937	31·9	
1938	1938–40 average,	1938–40 average,
1939	32·1	15·7
1940	36·4	15·6
1941	24·4	
1942	12·4	
1943	12·4	
1944	21·5	

	All grains	*Wheat*
1945	20·0	6·5
1946	17·5	6·1
1947	27·5	8·2
1948	30·2	13·3
1949	32·1	11·8
1950	32·3	15·1
1951	33·6	16·3
1952	34·7	20·8
1953	31·1	19·2
1954	34·6	19·9
1955	36·9	19·9
1956	54·1	37·2
1957	35·4	25·6
1958	56·6	41·9
1959	46·6	34·2
1960	46·7	30·7
1961	52·1	33·3
1962	56·6	34·6
1963	44·8	22·7
1964	68·3	38·7
1965	36·3	21·8
1966	75·0	56·8
1967	57·2	38·2
1968	69·0	49·0
1969	55·5	36·1
1970	73·3	51·0

Sources: *Istoriya, 1941–45*, 67–9
A. Malafeyev, *Istoriya Tsenoobrazovaniya v SSSR* (Moscow, 1964), 175, 177 (1928–33 figures)
Nar. Khoz. 1958, 357; *1963*, 273; *1969*, 323, 325; *1970*, 309, 311
Sel. Khoz. 1935, 240; *1960*, 196, 197; *1971*, 161
SSSR i Zarubezhnye Strany: stat. sbor. (1970), 95

60. **GRAIN** (continued)

3. Yields

(cn/ha)

		Wheat	
	All grains	*Winter*	*Spring*
1909–13 annual average	6·9	8·1	5·8
1913	8·1[x]	9·9[x]	7·3[xy]
	8·2[y]	10·0[y]	
1917	6·4		
1918	6·0		
1919	6·2		
1920	5·7		
1921	5·3	4·9	3·7
1922	8·5	9·8	7·2
1923	7·3	10·7	5·6
1924	6·2	7·4	5·2
1925	8·6	9·9	7·9
1926	8·4	10·0	7·7
1927	7·6	8·7	5·9
1928	7·9	7·8	8·0
1929	7·5	7·9	5·9
1930	8·5	10·6	7·3
1931	6·7	9·1	4·0
1932	7·0	7·4	5·1
1933			
1934	1933–7 average, 7·1	1933–7 average, 8·6	1933–7 average, 5·1
1935			
1936			
1937	9·3	11·5	8·3
1938	1938–40 average, 7·7	1938–40 average, 9·9	1938–40 average, 6·5
1939			
1940	8·6	10·1	6·6
1941	6·9		
1942	4·4		
1943	4·2		
1944	6·0		

60. GRAIN (continued)

3. Yields (continued)

(*cn/ha*)

	All grains	*Wheat* *Winter*	*Wheat* *Spring*
1945	5·6	6·3	4·8
1946	4·6	5·4	4·2
1947	7·3	7·5	6·3
1948	6·7	11·3	4·4
1949	6·9	7·8	5·7
1950	7·9	9·1	7·6
1951	7·4	10·9	5·7
1952	8·6	13·8	6·9
1953	7·8	11·1	7·0
1954	7·7	9·3	8·3
1955	8·4	13·5	5·3
1956	9·9	11·6	10·7
1957	8·4	14·7	6·1
1958	11·1	16·2	9·7
1959	10·4	15·2	9·4
1960	10·9	15·1	9·5
1961	10·7	16·9	8·2
1962	10·9	16·8	8·2
1963	8·3	12·9	5·9
1964	11·4	13·8	9·9
1965	9·5	16·1	5·5
1966	13·7	20·4	12·0
1967	12·1	17·8	8·9
1968	14·0	18·3	12·2
1969	13·2	18·9	10·1
1970	15·6	22·8	12·3

Sources: *Istoriya, 1941–45*, 67–9
Nar. Khoz. 1932, 121; *1958*, 418; *1961*, 304; *1963*, 273; *1964*, 252; *1968*, 321; *1969*, 323, 325; *1970*, 309, 311
Sel. Khoz. 1935, 239; *1960*, 208–9, 146, 197; *1971*, 161

61. COTTON

	Output (and state procure-ments) (m. tons)	*Average yield (cn/ha.)*		*Output (and state procure-ments) (m. tons)*	*Average yield (cn/ha.)*
1913	0·74	10·8	1945	1·2	9·6
			1946	1·6	12·6
1917	—	—	1947	1·7	11·6
1918	—	—	1948	2·2	13·9
1919	—	—	1949	2·5	14·4
1920	—	—	1950	3·5	15·3
1921	0·02	1·9	1951	3·7	13·7
1922	0·02	3·2	1952	3·8	13·3
1923	0·14	6·2	1953	3·9	20·5
1924	0·34	7·6	1954	4·2	19·1
1925	0·54	9·2	1955	3·9	17·7
1926	0·54	8·2	1956	4·3	21·0
1927	0·72	9·0	1957	4·2	20·1
1928	0·82	8·5	1958	4·3	20·2
1929	0·86	8·3	1959	4·6	21·6
1930	1·1	7·7	1960	4·3	19·6
1931	1·3	6·8	1961	4·5	19·3
1932	1·3	6·9	1962	4·3	18·0
1933	1·3	7·8	1963	5·2	21·0
1934	1·2	7·3	1964	5·3	21·5
1935	1·7	10·2	1965	5·7	23·2
1937	2·6	12·1	1966	6·0	24·3
1940	2·2	10·8	1967	6·0	24·5
			1968	5·9	24·3
			1969	5·7	22·5
			1970	6·9	25·1
			1971	over 7·0	

Note. The socialised sector has produced 100 per cent of cotton output consistently since 1940.

Sources: *Nar. Khoz. 1932*, 121; *1958*, 418; *1970*, 318
Pravda (23 January 1972) *Sel. Khoz.* (1935), 213

62. SUGAR BEET

	Output (m. tons)	Socialised sector (%)	State procurements (m. tons)	Average yield (cn/ha)
1913	11·3		—	168
1921	0·4			19
1922	1·9			106
1923	2·8			108
1924	3·5			92
1925	9·1			170
1926	6·4			118
1927	10·4			157
1928	10·1		9·4	132
1929	6·3		6·0	81
1930	14·0		13·2	135
1931	12·1		10·4	86
1932	6·6		6·1	64
1933	9·0		8·2	74
1934	11·4		9·5	96
1935	16·2		15·5	132
1937	21·6			181
1940	18·0	(94)	17·4	146
1945	5·5	(90)	4·7	66
1946	4·3		3·8	46
1947	14·0		12·2	129
1948	12·9		11·8	101
1949	15·7		15·3	121
1950	20·8	(100)	19·7	159
1951	23·6	(100)	23·4	170
1952	22·2	(100)	22·0	152
1953	23·2	(100)	22·9	148
1954	19·8	(100)	19·5	124

62. SUGAR BEET (continued)

	Output (m. tons)	Socialised sector (%)	State procurements (m. tons)	Average yield (cn/ha.)
1955	31·0	(100)	30·7	176
1956	32·5	(100)	31·5	162
1957	39·7	(100)	38·5	188
1958	54·4	(100)	51·0	218
1959	43·9	(100)	41·4	159
1960	57·7	(100)	52·2	191
1961	50·9	(100)	47·7	164
1962	47·4	(100)	43·9	152
1963	44·1	(100)	41·5	120
1964	81·2	(100)	76·1	199
1965	72·3	(100)	67·5	188
1966	74·0	(100)	69·7	195
1967	87·1	(100)	81·6	230
1968	94·3	(100)	84·2	266
1969	71·2	(100)	65·3	211
1970	78·3	(100)	71·4	237
1971	72·1			

Sources: *Nar. Khoz. 1932*, 121; *1958*, 418; *1961*, 304; *1964*, 259; *1968*, 321; *1970*, 320
Pravda (23 January 1972)
Sel. Khoz. (1935), 212–3, 215

63. FLAX (FIBRE)

	Output (000 tons)	State procurements (000 tons)	Average yield (cn/ha)
1913	330[x]	—	3·2
	401[y]		
1924	240		2·5
1925	300		2·4
1926	270		2·1
1927	240		2·0
1928	324	172	2·4
1929	361	227	2·2
1930	436	183	2·5
1931	553	256	2·3
1932	498	287	2·0
1933	548	255	2·3
1934	533	267	2·5
1935	550	295	2·6
1937	362		1·7
1940	349	245	1·7
1945	150	65	1·5
1946	133	75	1·4
1947	170	93	1·6
1948	257	162	1·9
1949	310	209	1·9
1950	255	174	1·3
1951	193	159	1·2
1952	213	189	1·4
1953	162	145	1·3
1954	218	192	2·0
1955	381	347	2·6
1956	521	427	2·7
1957	440	387	2·6
1958	438	392	2·7
1959	364	333	2·3

63. FLAX (FIBRE) (continued)

	Output (*000 tons*)	*State procurements* (*000 tons*)	*Average yield* (*cn/ha*)
1960	425	369	2·6
1961	399	369	2·5
1962	432	395	2·5
1963	380	368	2·6
1964	346	317	2·2
1965	480	433	3·3
1966	461	426	3·3
1967	485	447	3·5
1968	402	355	3·0
1969	487	447	3·7
1970	456	431	3·6

Sources: *Nar. Khoz. 1958*, 418; *1970*, 322
Sel. Khoz. (1935), 422
Sots. stroi. (1934), 211

64. SUNFLOWER SEED

	Output (000 tons)	*State procurements (000 tons)*	*Average yield (cn/ha)*
1913		—	7·6
1924	1300		5·0
1925	2230		7·2
1926	1550		6·0
1927	2160		7·6
1928	2127	1072	5·4
1929	1764	809	4·9
1930	1629	748	4·8
1931	2506	1351	5·5
1932	2268	563	4·3
1933	2354	797	6·0
1934	2077	702	5·9
1935	1850		5·6
1937	1755		5·4
1940	2636	1500	7·4
1945	844	490	2·9
1946	792	522	2·6
1947	1393	779	4·1
1948	1934	1135	5·6
1949	1852	1166	5·1
1950	1798	1084	5·0
1951	1739	1156	4·8
1952	2205	1346	6·0
1953	2630	1796	6·7
1954	1909	1188	4·7
1955	3797	2316	8·9
1956	3947	2391	8·7
1957	2801	1760	8·1
1958	4626	2615	11·8
1959	3019	1861	7·7

64. SUNFLOWER SEED (continued)

	Output (*000 tons*)	*State procurements* (*000 tons*)	*Average yield* (*cn/ha*)
1960	3967	2293	9·4
1961	4753	2923	11·2
1962	4795	3082	10·9
1963	4285	3035	9·7
1964	6058	3933	13·1
1965	5449	3888	11·1
1966	6150	4663	12·2
1967	6608	4867	13·8
1968	6685	4906	13·7
1969	6358	4312	13·3
1970	6144	4613	12·8
1971	5700		

Sources: *Nar. Khoz. 1958*, 418; *1970*, 324
Pravda (23 January 1972)
Sel. Khoz. (1935), 386
Sots. Stroi. (1934), 211

65. POTATOES

	Output (*m. tons*)	Socialised sector (%)	State procurements (*m. tons*)	Average yield (*cn/ha*)
1913	31·9[y]		—	66·6[x] 76[y]
1924	36·1		—	
1925	41·8		—	
1926	45·4		—	
1927			—	
1928	46·4		—	82
1929	45·6		—	80
1930	49·4		5·7	86
1931	44·8		6·9	73
1932	43·1		4·5	71
1933	49·3		5·7	87
1934	56·2		6·0	92
1935	69·7			95
1937	58·7			86
1940	76·1	(35)	8·5	99
1945	58·3	(25)	4·5	70
1946	55·6		4·6	73
1947	74·5		5·2	99
1948	95·0		7·2	109
1949	89·6		7·0	100
1950	88·6	(27)	6·9	104
1951	58·8		5·2	70
1952	69·2		5·6	84
1953	75·6	(28)	5·4	87
1954	75·0		6·6	86
1955	71·8		5·9	79
1956	96·0		9·2	104
1957	87·8		7·9	90
1958	86·5	(34)	7·0	91
1959	86·6	(37)	6·8	91

65. POTATOES (continued)

	Output (m. tons)	*Socialised sector (%)*	*State procurements (m. tons)*	*Average yield (cn/ha)*
1960	84·4	(37)	7·1	92
1961	84·3	(36)	7·0	95
1962	69·7	(30)	5·7	80
1963	71·8	(34)	8·0	84
1964	93·6	(40)	11·1	110
1965	88·7	(37)	9·9	103
1966	87·9	(36)	9·3	105
1967	95·5	(37)	11·7	115
1968	102·2	(38)	11·7	123
1969	91·8	(33)	10·6	113
1970	96·8	(35)	11·4	120
1971	92·3			

^{x} 1935 source; ^{y} 1969 source

Sources: *Nar. Khoz. 1958*, 418; *1961*, 304; *1964*, 252; *1968*, 321; *1969*, 340; *1970*, 281, 326
Pravda (23 January 1972)
Sel. Khoz. (1935), 467
Sots. Stroi. (1936), 339, 345
Ten Years of Soviet Power in Figures, 1917–1927, 119

66. VEGETABLES

	Output (*m. tons*)	Socialised sector (%)	State procurements (*m. tons*)	Average yield (*cn/ha*)
1913	4·4[x]			91[x]
	5·5[y]			84[y]
1928	10·5			132
1929	10·6			
1930	17·5			
1937	15·4			112
1940	13·7	(52)	3·0	91
1945	10·3	(44)	1·8	58
1946	8·9		1·5	54
1947	14·9		2·1	83
1948	13·2		2·0	82
1949	10·8		1·9	76
1950	9·3	(56)	2·0	72
1951	8·8		1·8	70
1952	9·8		1·8	78
1953	11·4	(52)	2·5	87
1954	11·9		3·0	82
1955	14·1		3·9	95
1956	14·3		3·8	91
1957	14·8		4·2	101
1958	14·9	(55)	4·2	101
1959	14·8	(54)	4·5	100
1960	16·6	(56)	5·1	111
1961	16·2	(55)	5·5	113
1962	16·0	(58)	6·2	109
1963	15·2	(59)	6·3	104
1964	19·5	(61)	7·9	130
1965	17·6	(59)	7·7	123
1966	17·9	(58)	8·0	125
1967	20·5	(60)	9·5	141
1968	19·0	(59)	9·1	131
1969	18·7	(61)	9·6	126
1970	20·3	(62)	10·9	138
1971	20			

[x] Pre-1939 territory; [y] Present territory

Sources: *Nar. Khoz. 1932*, 178–9; *1958*, 418; *1961*, 304; *1964*, 252; *1968*, 321; *1969*, 342; *1970*, 281, 328
Pravda (23 January 1972)

67. FRUIT AND BERRIES (INCLUDING GRAPES)

	Output (000 tons)	of which, grapes (000 tons)	State procurements (000 tons)	of which, grapes (000 tons)
1940	3873	1131	596	306
1945	2400	1130	275*	137
1950	2850	753	597	302
1953	3208	1036	1194	569
1956	3440	1220	1278	669
1957	4950	1400	1650	797
1958	4846	1734	1900	998
1959	4951	1734	1907	1035
1960	4942	1871	1951	1087
1961	5036	2225	2304	1405
1962	5978	2972	2937	1964
1963	6411	2572	3061	1786
1964	6866	2629	3415	1906
1965	8100	3723	4477	2875
1966	7805	3378	4473	2644
1967	8966	3441	4680	2605
1968	10,621	4472	6004	3531
1969	9467	4181	5817	3354
1970	11,690	4011	6180	3154

* 1945 figure excludes citrus fruits (which were 28,000 tons in 1940 and 45,000 in 1958).

Sources: *Nar. Khoz. 1959*, 314–15, 322–3; *1961*, 305, 379; *1964*, 336–7; *1967*, 410–11; *1969*, 351–3; *1970*, 337–8

68. TEA

Production (and procurements) of tea leaf
(000 tons)

1913	0·55
1928	1·06
1940	51·6
1950	84·9
1957	112
1958	138·2
1959	145·7
1960	163·7
1961	161·6
1962	178·9
1963	195·6
1964	193·7
1965	197·0
1966	238·2
1967	234·4
1968	229·0
1969	244·6
1970	272·7

Sources: *Nar. Khoz. 1958*, 440; *1961*, 380; *1964*, 337; *1967*, 411; *1969*, 353; *1970*, 338

69. TOBACCO

	Procurements		Production	
	Tobacco	Makhorka	Tobacco	Makhorka
	(000 tons)		(000 tons)	
1928			33	85
1929			32	87
1930			39	90
1931			53	116
1932			57	97
1933			55	93
1940	73	168		
1945	31	36		
1950	59	86		
1953	81	82		
1954	93	69		
1955	81	108		
1956	79	119		
1957	102	88		
1958	100	102		
1959	112	72		
1960	103	70		
1961	100	33		
1962	102	30		
1963	122	28		
1964	184	43		
1965	169	43		
1966	178	38		
1967	215	32		
1968	215	46		
1969	195	39		
1970	228	30		

Sources: *Nar. Khoz. 1932*, 178–9; *1958*, 357; *1961*, 305; *1964*, 255; *1967*, 337; *1969*, 299; *1970*, 285
Sel. Khoz. (1935), 459, 460

70. LIVESTOCK

(numbers at beginning of year, in millions)

	Cattle			*Cows*		
	Total	*State and collective (as % of total)*	*Private (as % of total)*	*Total*	*State and collective (as % of total)*	*Private (as % of total)*
1916	51·7[x]			24·9[x]		
	58·4[y]			28·8[y]		
1917	51·6			25·0		
1918	50·8			25·3		
1919	48·6			25·5		
1920	45·9			24·8		
1921	43·7			24·9		
1922	40·9			24·8		
1923	41·8			24·3		
1924	47·3			25·4		
1925	51·2			26·6		
1926	54·0			27·8		
1927	56·5			28·5		
1928	60·1	(0·5)*		29·3	(0·4)*	
	66·8[x]			33·2[y]		
1929	58·2	(0·9)*		29·2	(0·8)*	
1930	50·6	(8)*		28·5	(6)*	
1931	42·5	(23)*		24·5	(17)*	
1932	38·3	(34)*		22·3	(23)*	
1933	33·5	(35)*		19·4	(25)*	
1934	33·5	12·3 (37)	21·2 (63)	19·0	4·6 (24)*	14·4 (76)
1935	38·9	14·3 (37)	24·6 (63)	19·0	4·8 (25)	14·2 (75)
1936	46·0	17·5 (38)	28·5 (62)	20·0	5·1 (25)	14·9 (75)
1937	47·5	18·1 (38)	29·4 (62)	20·9	5·3 (25)	15·6 (75)
1938	50·9	18·0 (35)	32·9 (65)	22·7	5·5 (24)	17·2 (76)
1939	53·5	18·8 (35)	34·7 (65)	24·0	5·7 (24)	18·3 (76)
1940	47·8	20·9 (44)	26·9 (56)	22·8	6·2 (27)	16·6 (73)
1941	54·8	23·6 (43)	31·1 (57)	28·0	7·0 (25)	21·0 (75)

[x] Pre-1939 boundaries [y] Present boundaries.

* These figures relate to July of the respective years.

70. LIVESTOCK (continued)

(numbers at beginning of year, in millions)

	Cattle					Cows				
	Total	*State and collective*	*(as % of total)*	*Private*	*(as % of total)*	*Total*	*State and collective*	*(as % of total)*	*Private*	*(as % of total)*
1946	47·6	18·9	(40)	28·7	(60)	22·9	4·6	(20)	18·3	(80)
1947	47·0	18·7	(40)	28·3	(60)	23·0	4·6	(20)	18·4	(80)
1948	50·1	20·1	(40)	30·0	(60)	23·8	4·8	(20)	19·0	(80)
1949	54·8	24·5	(45)	30·3	(55)	24·2	5·7	(24)	18·5	(76)
1950	58·1	29·1	(50)	29·0	(50)	24·6	6·9	(30)	17·1	(70)
1951	57·1	32·3	(57)	24·8	(43)	24·3	8·3	(34)	16·0	(66)
1952	58·8	35·6	(61)	23·2	(39)	24·9	9·3	(37)	15·6	(63)
1953	56·6	34·5	(61)	22·1	(39)	24·3	9·9	(41)	14·4	(59)
1954	55·8	32·1	(58)	23·7	(42)	25·2	10·1	(40)	15·1	(60)
1955	56·7	31·3	(55)	25·4	(45)	26·4	11·2	(42)	15·2	(58)
1956	58·8	31·0	(53)	27·8	(47)	27·7	11·6	(42)	16·1	(58)
1957	61·4	32·5	(53)	28·9	(47)	29·0	12·6	(43)	16·4	(57)
1958	66·8	37·3	(56)	29·5	(44)	31·4	13·6	(43)	17·8	(57)
1959	70·8	41·3	(58)	29·5	(42)	33·3	14·7	(44)	18·6	(56)
1960	74·2	48·4	(65)	25·8	(35)	33·9	16·7	(49)	17·2	(51)
1961	75·8	52·7	(70)	23·0	(30)	34·8	18·5	(53)	16·3	(47)
1962	82·1	58·2	(71)	23·9	(29)	36·3	20·1	(55)	16·2	(45)
1963	87·0	62·5	(72)	24·5	(28)	38·0	21·8	(57)	16·2	(43)
1964	85·4	61·4	(72)	24·1	(28)	38·3	22·4	(58)	16·0	(42)
1965	87·2	62·1	(71)	25·1	(29)	38·8	22·6	(58)	16·2	(42)
1966	93·4	65·5	(70)	27·9	(30)	40·1	23·5	(59)	16·6	(41)
1967	97·1	67·8	(70)	29·3	(30)	41·2	24·1	(58)	17·1	(42)
1968	97·2	68·7	(71)	28·4	(29)	41·6	24·5	(59)	17·1	(41)
1969	95·7	68·5	(72)	27·3	(28)	41·2	24·4	(59)	16·7	(41)
1970	95·2	70·2	(74)	25·0	(26)	40·5	24·6	(61)	15·9	(39)
1971	99·2	74·3	(75)	24·9	(25)	41·0	25·5	(62)	15·5	(38)
1972	102·4	77·5	(76)	24·9	(24)	41·3	26·2	(63)	15·1	(37)

70. **LIVESTOCK** (continued)

(numbers at beginning of year, in millions)

	Sheep			Pigs		
	Total	*State and collective (as % of total)*	*Private (as % of total)*	*Total*	*State and collective (as % of total)*	*Private (as % of total)*
1916	82·5^{x} 89·7^{y}			17·3^{x} 23·0^{y}		
1917	81·7			18·6		
1918	80·2			19·3		
1919	78·7			18·4		
1920	77·3			16·3		
1921	75·7			15·4		
1922	68·2			13·1		
1923	62·9			10·4		
1924	69·1			14·6		
1925	78·6			18·4		
1926	85·8			18·1		
1927	90·3			18·7		
1928	97·3	(0·7)*†		22·0	(0·5)*	
	104·2^{y}			27·7^{y}		
1929	97·4	(1·3)*†		19·4	(0·9)*	
1930	85·5	(8)*†		14·2	(8)*	
1931	62·5	(22)*†		11·7	(25)*	
1932	43·8	(37)*†		10·9	(44)*	
1933	34·0	(41)*†		9·9	(49)*	
1934	32·9	15·7 (48)	17·2 (52)	11·5	6·2 (54)	5·3 (46)
1935	36·4	17·7 (49)	18·7 (51)	17·1	7·0 (41)	10·1 (59)
1936	43·8	22·4 (51)	21·4 (49)	25·9	9·2 (36)	16·7 (64)
1937	46·6	24·3 (52)	22·3 (48)	20·0	8·3 (41)	11·7 (59)
1938	57·3	28·0 (49)	29·3 (51)	25·7	8·8 (34)	16·9 (66)
1939	69·9	32·6 (47)	37·3 (53)	25·2	9·1 (38)	16·1 (64)
1940	66·6	37·9 (57)	28·7 (43)	22·5	9·7 (43)	12·8 (57)
1941	80·0	46·2 (58)	33·8 (42)	27·6	11·5 (42)	16·1 (58)

^{x} Pre-1939 boundaries ^{y} Present boundaries.

* These figures relate to July of the respective year.

† Includes goats.

70. LIVESTOCK (continued)

(numbers at beginning of year, in millions)

	Sheep Total	Sheep State and collective	(as % of total)	Sheep Private	(as % of total)	Pigs Total	Pigs State and collective	(as % of total)	Pigs Private	(as % of total)
1946	58·5	38·6	(66)	19·9	(34)	10·6	4·3	(41)	6·3	(59)
1947	57·7	40·4	(70)	17·3	(30)	8·7	4·0	(46)	4·7	(54)
1948	63·3	45·2	(71)	18·1	(29)	9·7	4·9	(51)	4·8	(49)
1949	70·4	52·4	(74)	18·0	(26)	15·2	7·8	(51)	7·4	(49)
1950	77·6	61·5	(79)	16·1	(21)	22·2	12·7	(57)	9·5	(43)
1951	82·6	69·4	(84)	13·2	(16)	24·4	15·9	(65)	8·5	(35)
1952	90·5	76·5	(85)	14·0	(15)	27·1	19·4	(72)	7·7	(28)
1953	94·3	82·1	(87)	12·2	(13)	28·5	20·1	(71)	8·4	(29)
1954	99·8	84·8	(85)	15·0	(15)	33·3	17·8	(53)	15·5	(47)
1955	99·0	80·4	(82)	18·6	(18)	30·9	15·0	(49)	15·9	(51)
1956	103·3	81·7	(79)	21·6	(21)	34·0	17·1	(50)	16·9	(50)
1957	108·2	84·6	(78)	23·6	(22)	40·8	22·9	(56)	17·9	(44)
1958	120·2	94·1	(78)	26·1	(22)	44·3	29·2	(66)	15·1	(34)
1959	129·9	100·8	(78)	29·1	(22)	48·7	33·1	(68)	15·6	(32)
1960	136·1	106·6	(78)	29·5	(22)	53·4	38·4	(72)	15·0	(28)
1961	133·0	105·0	(79)	28·1	(21)	58·7	43·3	(74)	15·4	(26)
1962	137·5	107·9	(78)	29·6	(22)	66·7	49·4	(74)	17·3	(26)
1963	139·7	109·7	(79)	29·9	(21)	70·0	53·9	(77)	16·1	(23)
1964	133·9	107·4	(80)	26·5	(20)	40·9	27·7	(68)	13·2	(32)
1965	125·2	99·3	(79)	26·0	(21)	52·8	38·4	(73)	14·5	(27)
1966	129·8	102·2	(79)	27·6	(21)	59·6	41·3	(69)	18·2	(31)
1967	135·5	106·9	(79)	28·6	(21)	58·0	41·5	(72)	16·5	(28)
1968	138·4	109·5	(79)	28·9	(21)	50·9	37·3	(73)	13·6	(27)
1969	140·6	110·9	(79)	29·7	(21)	49·0	36·3	(74)	12·8	(26)
1970	130·7	103·3	(79)	27·4	(21)	56·1	42·2	(75)	13·8	(25)
1971	138·0	109·2	(79)	28·8	(21)	67·5	50·9	(75)	16·6	(25)
1972						71·4	55·6	(78)	15·8	(22)

70. LIVESTOCK (continued)

(numbers at beginning of year, in millions)

	Goats Total	Goats State and collective	(as % of total)	Goats Private	(as % of total)	Horses Total	Horses State and collective	(as % of total)	Horses Private	(as % of total)
1916	6·2x					35·8x				
	6·6y					38·2y				
1917	6·3					34·5				
1918	6·5					33·9				
1919	6·4					32·3				
1920	6·2					30·3				
1921	6·1					28·7				
1922	5·5					25·7				
1923	5·1					23·3				
1924	5·4					24·0				
1925	6·0					25·2				
1926	7·3					26·9				
1927	9·0					29·1				
1928	9·7					32·1		(0·7)*		
	10·4y					36·1y				
1929	9·7					32·6		(1·4)*		
1930	7·8					31·0		(15)*		
1931	5·6					27·0		(49)*		
1932	3·8					21·7		(59)*		
1933	3·3					17·3		(70)*		
1934	3·6	0·6	(17)	3·0	(83)	15·4	11·1	(72)	4·3	(28)
1935	4·4	0·7	(16)	3·7	(84)	14·9	12·0	(80)	2·9	(20)
1936	6·1	0·9	(15)	5·2	(85)	15·5	13·6	(88)	1·9	(12)
1937	7·2	1·1	(15)	6·1	(85)	15·9	14·2	(89)	1·7	(11)
1938	9·3	1·3	(14)	8·0	(86)	16·2	14·5	(90)	1·7	(10)
1939	11·0	1·5	(14)	9·5	(86)	17·2	15·6	(91)	1·6	(9)
1940	10·1	2·2	(22)	7·9	(78)	17·7	16·6	(94)	1·1	(6)
1941	11·7	2·9	(25)	8·8	(75)	21·1	17·0	(81)	4·1	(19)

x Pre-1939 boundaries y Present boundaries.
* These figures relate to July of the respective year.

70. LIVESTOCK (continued)

(numbers at beginning of year, in millions)

	Goats					Horses				
	Total	*State and collective*	*(as % of total)*	*Private*	*(as % of total)*	*Total*	*State and collective*	*(as % of total)*	*Private*	*(as % of total)*
1946	11·5	4·5	(39)	7·0	(61)	10·7	8·2	(77)	2·5	(23)
1947	11·6	5·1	(44)	6·5	(56)	10·9	8·4	(77)	2·5	(23)
1948	13·5	5·6	(41)	7·9	(59)	11·0	8·6	(78)	2·4	(22)
1949	15·2	6·2	(41)	9·0	(59)	11·8	9·8	(83)	2·0	(17)
1950	16·0	7·2	(45)	8·8	(55)	12·7	11·7	(92)	1·0	(8)
1951	16·4	7·7	(48)	8·6	(52)	13·8	13·3	(96)	0·5	(4)
1952	17·1	7·1	(42)	10·0	(58)	14·7	14·3	(97)	0·4	(3)
1953	15·6	5·5	(35)	10·1	(65)	15·3	15·0	(98)	0·3	(2)
1954	15·7	4·2	(27)	11·5	(73)	15·3	14·8	(97)	0·5	(3)
1955	14·0	2·9	(21)	11·1	(79)	14·2	13·6	(96)	0·6	(4)
1956	12·9	2·1	(16)	10·8	(84)	13·0	12·4	(95)	0·6	(5)
1957	11·6	1·7	(15)	9·9	(85)	12·4	11·8	(95)	0·6	(5)
1958	9·9	1·6	(16)	8·3	(84)	11·9	11·3	(95)	0·6	(5)
1959	9·3	1·5	(16)	7·8	(84)	11·5	10·9	(95)	0·6	(5)
1960	7·9	1·5	(19)	6·4	(81)	11·0	10·4	(95)	0·6	(5)
1961	7·3	1·3	(18)	6·0	(82)	9·9				
1962	7·0	1·2	(17)	5·8	(83)	9·4				
1963	6·7	1·1	(16)	5·6	(84)	9·1				
1964	5·6	1·1	(20)	4·6	(80)	8·5				
1965	5·5	0·9	(16)	4·5	(84)	7·9				
1966	5·5	0·9	(16)	4·7	(84)	8·0				
1967	5·5	0·9	(16)	4·7	(84)	8·0				
1968	5·6	0·9	(16)	4·7	(84)	8·0				
1969	5·5	0·9	(16)	4·6	(84)	8·0				
1970	5·1	0·9	(18)	4·2	(82)	7·5				
1971	5·4	1·0	(19)	4·4	(81)	7·4				

Sources: *Nar. Khoz. 1961*, 381, 382–3; *1964*, 353–4; *1968*, 394–5; *1969*, 367–9; *1970*, 353
Sel. Khoz. (1935), 511; (1960), 263, 264
Sotsialisticheskoe Stroitel'stvo SSSR (1936), 354
SSSR i Zarubezhnye Strany: stat. sbor. (1970), 99
Pravda (23 January 1972)

71. MEAT

	Total production (m. tons) (slaughter weight)	Collective and state farm production (m. tons)	(as % of total)	Private production (m. tons)	State procurements (m. tons) (live weight)		(slaughter weight)
1913	4·1[x]						
	5·0[y]						
1917	4·3						
1918						0·1	
1921	3·3						
1924	3·4					0·4	
1928	4·9		(0·5)		1928–32 ave. per year, 2·1		
1929	5·8						
1930	4·3						
1931	3·9						
1932	2·8		(32)			1·2	
1933	2·3				1933–7 ave. per year, 1·1	0·9	
1934	2·0					1·1	
1935	2·3						
1936	3·7						
1937	3·0					1·3	
1938	4·5				1938–40 ave. per year, 2·2		
1939	5·1						
1940	3·9[x]						
	4·7[y]	1·3	(28)	3·4		2·2	1·3

[x] Pre-1939 boundaries [y] Present boundaries.

71. MEAT (continued)

	Total production (m. tons) (slaughter weight)	Collective and state farm production (m. tons)	(as % of total)	Private production (m. tons)	State procurements (m. tons) (live weight)	(slaughter weight)
1945	2·6	1·0	(39)	1·6	1·3	
1946	3·1	1·1	(34)	2·0	1·4	
1947	2·5	0·9	(39)	1·6	1·4	
1948	3·1	1·0	(32)	2·1	1·7	
1949	3·8	1·2	(31)	2·6	1·8	
1950	4·9	1·6	(33)	3·3	2·3	1·3
1951	4·7	1·8	(39)	2·9	2·6	
1952	5·2	2·3	(43)	2·9	3·2	
1953	5·8	2·8	(48)	3·0	3·6	2·1
1954	6·3	2·7	(44)	3·6	4·0	
1955	6·3	3·0	(46)	3·3	4·2	
1956	6·6	3·0	(45)	3·6	4·4	
1957	7·4	3·4	(47)	4·0	5·1	
1958	7·7	3·7	(48)	4·0	5·7	3·4
1959	8·7	4·8	(53)	3·9	7·5	4·6
1960	8·7	5·1	(59)	3·6	7·9	4·8
1961	8·7	4·8	(55)	3·9	7·3	4·5
1962	9·5	5·3	(56)	4·2	8·6	5·3
1963	10·2	5·9	(58)	4·3	9·3	5·7
1964	8·3	4·8	(58)	3·5	8·3	5·0
1965	10·0	6·0	(60)	4·0	9·3	5·8
1966	10·7	6·3	(59)	4·4	10·3	6·5
1967	11·5	7·0	(61)	4·5	11·5	7·2
1968	11·6	7·2	(62)	4·4	11·9	7·4
1969	11·8	7·6	(64)	4·2	11·7	7·4
1970	12·3	8·0	(65)	4·3	12·6	8·1
1971	13·1				14·1	9·2

Sources: *Nar. Khoz. 1961*, 305; *1964*, 369; *1968*, 405; *1969*, 298, 373, 379; *1970*, 357, 362, 365
Pravda (23 January 1972)
Sel. 'khoz (1935), 524; (1960), 93, 328–9, 330
SSSR i Zarubezhnye strany: stat. sbor. (1970), 94, 96, 99

	Total production (m. tons)	Collective and state farm production (m. tons)	Collective and state farm production (as % of total)	Private production (m. tons)	State procurements (m. tons)	Average annual yield per cow (kg): Overall	Average annual yield per cow (kg): Collective and state farms
1913	24·1[x] 28·8[y]						
1917	24·2						
1918					0·2		
1921	19·2						
1924	26·2				0·7		
1928	31·0		(0·6)		1928–32 annual average: 1·7		
1929	29·8						
1930	27·0						
1931	23·4						
1932	20·6		(22)				
1933	19·2				1933–7 annual average: 4·3		
1934	20·8						962
1935	21·4						
1936	23·5						
1937	26·1				5·0		
1938	29·0				1938–40 annual average: 5·6		
1939	27·2						

72. **MILK** (continued)

	Total production (m. tons)	Collective and state farm production (m. tons)	Collective and state farm production (as % of total)	Private production (m. tons)	State procurements (m. tons)	Average annual yield per cow (kg): Overall	Average annual yield per cow (kg): Collective and state farms
1940	26·6[x]						
	33·6[y]	7·5	(23)	26·1	6·5	1185	1124
1945	26·4	4·7	(18)	21·7	2·9		987
1946	27·7	4·9	(17)	22·8	4·9		968
1947	30·2	5·1	(17)	25·1	5·3		1033
1948	33·4	6·3	(19)	27·1	6·7		1148
1949	34·9	7·6	(22)	27·3	7·5		1164
1950	35·3	8·9	(25)	26·4	8·5	1370	1137
1951	36·2	10·4	(29)	25·8	9·4		1148
1952	35·7	11·2	(31)	24·5	10·1		1129
1953	36·5	12·1	(33)	24·4	10·6	1389	1157
1954	38·2	13·5	(35)	24·7	11·3		1201
1955	43·0	17·0	(40)	26·0	13·5		1422
1956	49·1	21·3	(44)	27·8	17·3		1693
1957	54·7	25·3	(46)	29·4	20·5		1930
1958	58·7	27·6	(47)	31·1	22·1	1755	1994
1959	61·7	31·4	(51)	30·3	25·0		2067

1960	61·7	32·6	(53)	29·1	26·3	1779	1938
1961	62·6	34·1	(54)	28·5	27·5	1744	1847
1962	63·9	35·2	(55)	28·7	29·2	1693	1747
1963	61·2	33·9	(55)	27·3	28·5	1600	1584
1964	63·3	36·3	(57)	27·0	31·4	1655	1684
1965	72·6	43·9	(60)	28·7	38·7	1853	1987
1966	76·0	45·8	(60)	30·2	40·1	1880	2021
1967	79·9	48·8	(61)	31·1	42·5	1948	2128
1968	82·3	51·0	(62)	31·3	44·0	2026	2229
1969	81·5	51·2	(63)	30·3	43·8	2056	2249
1970	83·0	53·2	(64)	29·8	45·7	2110	2298
1971	83·3				47·1		

[x] Pre-1939 boundaries [y] Present boundaries.

Sources: *Nar. Khoz. 1959*, 320; *1961*, 407; *1964*, 373; *1968*, 408; *1969*, 298, 373; *1970*, 357, 362, 367, 368
Pravda (23 January 1972)
Sel. Khoz. (1935), 563; (1960), 93, 328–9, 330
SSSR i Zarubezhnye Strany: stat. sbor. (1970), 94, 96, 99

73. EGGS

	Total production (mlrd)	Collective and state farm production (mlrd)	(as % of total)	Private production (mlrd)	State procurements (mlrd)
1913	10·2[x]				
	11·9[y]				
1917	9·5				
1918					0·09
1924	6·7				0·8
1928	10·8		(0·1)		
1929	10·1				
1930	8·0				1928–32 annual average 1·4
1931	6·7				
1932	4·4		(6)		
1933	3·5				
1934	4·2				
1935	5·8				1933–7 annual average 0·8
1936	7·4				
1937	8·2				1·4
1938	10·5				
1939	11·5				1938–40 annual average 2·2
1940	10·2[x]				
	12·2[y]	0·7	(6)	11·5	2·7

[x] Pre-1939 boundaries [y] Present boundaries.

73. EGGS (continued)

	Total production (mlrd)	Collective and state farm production (mlrd)	(as % of total)	Private production (mlrd)	State procurements (mlrd)
1945	4·9	0·5	(10)	4·4	1·1
1946	5·2	0·5	(9)	4·7	1·2
1947	4·9	0·4	(8)	4·5	0·7
1948	6·6	0·5	(8)	6·1	1·1
1949	9·1	0·9	(10)	8·2	1·4
1950	11·7	1·3	(11)	10·4	1·9
1951	13·3	1·7	(13)	11·6	2·3
1952	14·4	2·0	(14)	12·4	2·4
1953	16·1	2·5	(15)	13·6	2·6
1954	17·2	2·2	(14)	15·0	2·7
1955	18·5	2·3	(13)	16·2	2·9
1956	19·5	2·5	(13)	17·0	3·3
1957	22·3	3·1	(14)	19·2	4·3
1958	23·0	3·4	(15)	19·6	4·5
1959	25·2	4·5	(18)	20·7	5·7
1960	27·4	5·3	(19)	22·1	6·5
1961	29·3	6·3	(22)	23·0	7·4
1962	30·1	7·1	(24)	23·0	8·5
1963	28·5	7·1	(25)	21·4	8·7
1964	26·7	7·0	(26)	19·7	8·3
1965	29·1	9·5	(33)	19·6	10·5
1966	31·7	10·8	(34)	20·9	11·6
1967	33·9	12·6	(37)	21·3	12·9
1968	35·7	14·5	(41)	21·2	14·1
1969	37·2	16·3	(44)	20·9	15·4
1970	40·7	19·0	(47)	21·7	18·1
1971	44·9				21·6

Sources: *Nar. Khoz. 1959*, 320; *1970*, 357, 362
Pravda (23 January 1972)
Sel. Khoz. (1960), 93, 328–9, 330
SSSR i Zarubezhnye Strany. stat. sbor. (1970), 94, 96, 99

74. WOOL

	Total production (000 tons)	Collective and state farm production (000 tons)	Collective and state farm production (as % of total)	Private production (000 tons)	State procurements (000 tons) (accounting weight)		Average yield per sheep (kg/sheep/annum) Overall	Average yield per sheep (kg/sheep/annum) Kolkhozy and sovkhozy
1913	180[x]							
	192[y]							
1917	154							
1921	113							
1924	130							
1928	182		(1·5)					
1929	183				1928–32			
1930	141				annual	45		
1931	98				average			
1932	69		(42)					1·9 (*kolkhozy*)
1933	64							
1934	65				1933–7			
1935	79				annual	57		2·5
1936	99				average			
1937	106							
1938	137				1938–40			
1939	150				annual average	106		

1940	151[x] 161[y]	98	(61)	63	120	2·2	2·5
1945	111	75	(68)	36	67		1·9
1946	119	81	(69)	38	74		2·0
1947	125	90	(72)	35	84		2·2
1948	146	106	(73)	40	96		2·3
1949	163	123	(75)	40	120		2·3
1950	180	141	(79)	39	136	2·2	2·2
1951	192	156	(81)	36	153		2·2
1952	219	182	(83)	37	182		2·3
1953	235	199	(85)	36	197	2·4	2·4
1954	230	191	(83)	39	190		2·2
1955	256	207	(81)	49	230		2·6
1956	261	205	(79)	56	246		2·5
1957	289	228	(79)	61	281		2·7
1958	322	253	(78)	69	315	2·7	2·7
1959	355	278	(79)	77	354		2·7
1960	357	279	(78)	78	358	2·6	2·6
1961	366	288	(79)	78	369	2·7	2·7
1962	371	289	(78)	82	374	2·7	2·7
1963	373	294	(79)	79	380	2·7	2·7
1964	341	270	(79)	71	353	2·5	2·5

74. WOOL (continued)

	Total production (000 tons)	Collective and state farm production (000 tons)	Collective and state farm production (as % of total)	Private production (000 tons)	State procurements (000 tons) (accounting weight)	Average yield per sheep (kg/sheep/annum) Overall	Average yield per sheep (kg/sheep/annum) Kolkhozy and sovkhozy
1965	357	284	(80)	73	368	2·8	2·9
1966	371	295	(80)	76	380	2·9	2·9
1967	395	315	(80)	80	410	2·9	3·0
1968	415	332	(80)	83	429	3·0	3·0
1969	390	307	(79)	83	402	2·8	2·8
1970	419	337	(80)	82	441	3·2	3·3
1971	424						

[x] Pre-1939 boundaries [y] Present boundaries.

Note. Wool procurements are given in accounting weight, which is reached by converting the physical weight according to zonal norms of the amount of pure fibre obtained from unwashed wool. For example, if a *kolkhoz* has sold to the state 800 kg of wool, with a yield of pure fibre of 38%, when the norm is 35%, the accounting weight is 869 kg (*Nar. Khoz. 1969*, 299n).

Sources: *Nar. Khoz. 1958*, 357; *1959*, 408; *1961*, 407; *1964*, 366, 373; *1968*, 408; *1969*, 373, 377, 382; *1970*, 357, 362, 367, 369
Pravda (23 January 1972)
Sel. Khoz. (1960), 328–9, 330, 111, 369–70, 93
SSSR i Zarubezhnye Strany: stat. sbor. (1970), 96, 99

Soviet Sources Used

Bol'shaya Sovetskaya Entsiklopediya, 2nd ed, vol. 29 ('National Income')

Dostizheniya Sovetskoi Vlasti za 40 let v tsifrakh, Statisticheskii sbornik (Gosstatizdat: Moscow, 1957)

Gosudarstvennyi Byudzhet SSSR, Statisticheskii sbornik (Finansy: Moscow, 1966)

Istoriya Velikoi Otechestvennoi Voiny, 1941–45, vol. VI (Moscow, 1965)

Kapital'noe Stroitel'stvo v SSSR, Statisticheskii sbornik (Gosstatizdat: Moscow, 1961)

Kul'turnoe Stroitel'stvo SSSR, Statisticheskii sbornik (Gosstatizdat: Moscow, 1956)

A. Malafeyev, *Istoriya Tsenoobrazovaniya v SSSR* (Moscow, 1964)

Narodnoe Khozyaistvo SSSR v 1932, Statisticheskii spravochnik (Gos. Sots-ekon. iz.: Moscow, Leningrad, 1932)

Narodnoe Khozyaistvo SSSR v 1958, Statisticheskii ezhegodnik (Gosstatizdat: Moscow, 1959)

Narodnoe Khozyaistvo SSSR v 1959, Statisticheskii ezhegodnik (Gosstatizdat: Moscow, 1960)

Narodnoe Khozyaistvo SSSR v 1960, Statisticheskii ezhegodnik (Gosstatizdat: Moscow, 1961)

Narodnoe Khozyaistvo SSSR v 1961, Statisticheskii ezhegodnik (Gosstatizdat: Moscow, 1962)

Narodnoe Khozyaistvo SSSR v 1962, Statisticheskii ezhegodnik (Gosstatizdat: Moscow, 1963)

Narodnoe Khozyaistvo SSSR v 1963, Statisticheskii ezhegodnik (Statistika: Moscow, 1965)

Narodnoe Khozyaistvo SSSR v 1964, Statisticheskii ezhegodnik (Statistika: Moscow, 1965)

Narodnoe Khozyaistvo SSSR v 1965, Statisticheskii ezhegodnik (Statistika: Moscow, 1966)

Narodnoe Khozyaistvo SSSR v 1967, Statisticheskii ezhegodnik (Statistika: Moscow, 1968)

Narodnoe Khozyaistvo SSSR v 1968, Statisticheskii ezhegodnik (Statistika: Moscow, 1969)

Narodnoe Khozyaistvo SSSR v 1969, Statisticheskii ezhegodnik (Statistika: Moscow, 1970)

Narodnoe Khozyaistvo SSSR v 1970, Statisticheskii ezhegodnik (Statistika: Moscow, 1971)

Promyshlennost' SSSR, Statisticheskii sbornik (Gosstatizdat: Moscow, 1957)

Promyshlennost' SSSR, Statisticheskii sbornik (Statistika: Moscow, 1964)

Sel'skoe Khozyaistvo SSSR, ezhegodnik, 1935 (Sel'khozgiz: Moscow, 1936)

Sel'skoe Khozyaistvo SSSR, Statisticheskii sbornik (Gosstatizdat: Moscow, 1960)

Sel'skoe Khozyaisto SSSR, Statisticheskii sbornik, (Statistika: Moscow, 1971)

Sotsialisticheskoe Stroitel'stvo Soyuza SSSR (*1933–1938 gg*), Statisticheskii sbornik (Gosplanizdat: Moscow, 1939)

Sotsialisticheskoe Stroitel'stvo SSSR, Statisticheskii ezhegodnik (TsUNKhU Gosplana SSSR: Moscow, 1934)

Sotsialisticheskoe Stroitel'stvo SSSR, Statisticheskii ezhegodnik (TsUNKhU Gosplana SSSR: Moscow, 1935)

Sotsialisticheskoe Stroitel'stvo SSSR, Statisticheskii ezhegodnik (TsUNKhU Gosplana SSSR: Moscow, 1936)

Sovetskaya Torgovlya, Statisticheskii sbornik (Gosstatizdat: Moscow, 1956)

SSSR i Zarubezhnye Strany, posle pobedy velikoi oktyabr'skoi sotsialisticheskoi revolyutsii: Statisticheskii sbornik (Statistika: Moscow, 1970)

Strana Sovetov za 50 let, Sbornik statisticheskikh materialov (Statistika: Moscow, 1967)

Ten Years of Soviet Power in Figures, 1917–27 (Central Statistics Board USSR, 1927)

Trud v SSSR, Statisticheskii spravochnik (TsUNKhU Gosplana SSSR: Moscow, 1936)

Trud v SSSR, Statisticheskii sbornik (Statistika: Moscow, 1968)

Vneshnaya Torgovlya SSSR za 1918–40, Statisticheskii sbornik (Vneshtorgizdat, Moscow, 1960)

Vneshnaya Torgovlya SSSR za 1918–66, Statisticheskii sbornik (Izdatel'stvo Mezhdunarodnye otnosheniya, Moscow, 1967)

Vneshnaya Torgovlya SSSR za 1955–59, Statisticheskii sbornik (Vneshtorgizdat, Moscow, 1961)

Vneshnaya Torgovlya SSSR za 1959–63, Statisticheskii sbornik (Vneshtorgizdat, Moscow, 1965)
Vneshnaya Torgovlya SSSR za 1964,* Statisticheskii sbornik (Vneshtorgizdat, Moscow, 1965)
Vneshnaya Torgovlya SSSR za 1966,* Statisticheskii sbornik (Vneshtorgizdat, Moscow, 1967)
Vneshnaya Torgovlya SSSR za 1968,* Statisticheskii sbornik (Vneshtorgizdat, Moscow, 1969)
Vneshnaya Torgovlya SSSR za 1970,* Statisticheskii sbornik (Vneshtorgizdat, Moscow, 1971)
Vysshee Obrazovanie v SSSR, Statisticheskii sbornik (Gosstatizdat: Moscow, 1961)
Zdravookhranenie v SSSR, Statisticheskii sbornik (Gosstatizdat: Moscow, 1960)

On the reliability of Soviet statistics, the following are useful:

A. Nove, *The Soviet Economy*, Appendix. A note on the Availability and Reliability of Soviet Statistics (all editions)
V. G. Treml and J. P. Hardt, *Soviet Economic Statistics*

* These volumes appear annually, giving data for the last two years. It is therefore only necessary to use alternate annual volumes in order to compile an annual series.

APPENDIX

Targets of Ninth Five-year (1971–5) Plan

1. National aggregates

	(as % of 1970)				
	1971	*1972*	*1973*	*1974*	*1975*
National income (utilised, in constant 1965 prices)	106·1	112·8	120·9	129	138·6
Industrial production	106·9	115·4	124·4	135·1	147
Producer goods	106·7	115·3	124·1	134·7	146·3
Consumer goods	107·4	115·7	125·1	136	148·6
State investment	106·5	112·8	124	132·5	139·6
Transport turnover	105·3	111·6	118·3	126	135·1
Labour productivity in industry	105·9	113	120·3	129	138·8
Labour productivity in construction	106·4	113·2	120·6	128·5	137
Labour productivity in rail transport	103·7	108·1	112·7	117·5	122·6
Profit from industry	113	127	143·8	164·7	190·4
State and co-operative retail trade turnover	106·4	114·6	123·3	132·3	141·8
Social consumption fund	107·2	114·1	121·1	130·5	140·6
Increase in real income per capita	104·7	111	117·3	123·8	130·8
Average monthly wage of state-employed labour force	102·8	107·5	112·3	117·5	122·4*
Services supplied to population	116·7	131·7	151·4	173·8	200·3
Number of children in pre-school institutions financed by state budget	104	108·3	113·5	118·8	124·6
Number of children in schools and groups with extended day	105·8	112·1	119·1	126	132·3
Entry of students to higher education	100·3	101	101·7	104·3	108
Entry of students to secondary specialised education	100	101·7	102·2	104·9	108·8
Entry of students to professional technical education	103·7	106	110·4	116	122·9
Number of hospital beds	102·2	105	107·3	109·8	112·6

* Almost 150 rubles.

Source: *Pravda* (25 and 27 November 1971)

2. Industrial production

	1971	*1972*	*1973*	*1974*	*1975*
Electricity (mlrd kwh)	790	850	913	985	1065
Oil (m. tons)	371	395	429	461	496
Natural gas (mlrd cubic metres)	211	229	250	280	320
Coal (m. tons)	620	634	652	670	695
Steel (m. tons)	120	126	131	138	146
Output of chemical and petro-chemical industry (mlrd rubles)	22·8	25·2	27·9	31·7	36·3
Plastics and synthetic resins (000 tons)	1785	1992	2277	2759	3533
Chemical fibres (000 tons)	672	746	828	911	1065
Cellulose (000 tons)	5447	5812	6637	7496	8490
Paper (000 tons)	4362	4556	4855	5174	5564
Cement (m. tons)	99	103·4	108·5	116·3	125
Engineering and metal-working output (mlrd rubles)	93	104	116	130	146
Vehicles (000)	1122	1376	1703	1987	2100
of which, cars (000)	513	728	977	1204	1260
Instruments, means of automation, and spare parts for them (m. rubles)	3310	3868	4487	5359	6308
Machinery and equipment for light and food industry (m. rubles)	825	934	1127	1338	1576
Agricultural machinery (m. rubles)	2336	2641	2978	3324	3702
Tractors (000)	470	478	502	542	575
(million horse power)	31·6	34	42·7	49·3	53
Grain combines (000)	102	103	94	123	138
Furniture (mlrd rubles)	2·99	3·34	3·68	4·086	4·63
Refrigerators (000)	4568	5131	5782	6288	6901
Fabrics (mlrd square metres)	9·4	9·6	10·06	10·45	11·1
Leather footwear (m. pairs)	708	728	759	791	830
Mineral fertiliser (m. tons)					90
Housing (m. square metres completed)					580*

Source: *Pravda* (25 November 1971)
* for five years ending in 1975.

3. Investment

	in 5 years ending in 1970 (actual)	*1975 (plan)*
Total investment (mlrd rubles)	354	501
Agricultural investment	—	almost 129

Source: *Pravda* (25 November 1971)

4. Regional growth

(1975 as % of 1970)

	Total industrial production	*Agricultural production (1971–5 as % of 1965–70)*	*Retail turnover*
RSFSR	147	122	139
Ukraine	143	119	143
Belorussia	158	125	148
Uzbekistan	151	124	152
Kazakhstan	159	122	144
Georgia	144	127	153
Azerbaidjan	146	135	156
Lithuania	149	116	143
Moldavia	162	136	146
Latvia	140	119	138
Kirghizia	155	120	151
Tadjikistan	138	128	147
Armenia	164	132	175
Turkmenia	164	120	152
Estonia	138	120	132

Source: *Pravda* (27 November 1971)

5. Agricultural production

Gross output (1971–5 as % of 1966–70)	120–122
Grain (m. tons, average 1971–5)	195
Cotton (m. tons, average 1971–5)	7·1
Meat (dead weight, m. tons, average 1971–5)	14·3
Meat (dead weight, m. tons, 1975)	15·6
Milk (m. tons, average 1971–5)	92·3
(m. tons, 1975)	98
Eggs (mlrd, average 1971–5)	46·7
(mlrd, 1975)	51
Wool (000 tons, average 1971–5)	464

6. Deliveries of supplies

	1975
Fertiliser (m. tons)	72
	1971–5 total
Tractors (000)	1700
Lorries (000)	1100
Grain combines (000)	541

Sources: *Pravda* (3 July 1970); (14 February 1971)

7. Procurements

	1975
Grain (m. tons)	60·0*
Cotton (m. tons)	6·8
Sugar beet (m. tons)	82·0
Sunflower seed (m. tons)	5·9
Flax (000 tons)	520·0
Potatoes (m. tons)	15·5
Vegetables (m. tons)	19·0
Fruit and berries (m. tons)	5·0
Grapes (m. tons)	5·4
Meat and poultry (live weight, m. tons)	16·0
Milk (m. tons)	55·0
Eggs (mlrd)	26·0
Wool (000 tons)	47·0

* But 30% overfulfilment 'expected as a minimum', at 50% premium prices.

Note. The targets for agricultural production, procurements and deliveries of supplies were not given in the final version of the Plan; however, enough of the figures from the drafts were repeated to indicate that these figures were unchanged.

Source: *Pravda* (3 July 1970)